THE SHORTER LEIBNIZ TEXTS

Also available from Continuum

Leibniz Reinterpreted, Lloyd Strickland

Leibniz: A Guide for the Perplexed, Franklin Perkins

THE SHORTER LEIBNIZ TEXTS

A Collection of New Translations

Lloyd Strickland

Continuum

The Tower Building
11 York Road
London SE1 7NX

80 Maiden Lane, Suite 704
New York, NY 10038

British Library Cataloguing-in-Publication Data
A catalogue record for this book is available from the British Library.

ISBN: 0826489508 (hardback) 0826489516 (paperback)

Library of Congress Cataloging-in-Publication Data

A catalog record for this book is available from the Library of Congress.

Typeset by Interactive Sciences Ltd, Gloucester
Printed and bound in Great Britain by Cromwell Press Ltd, Trowbridge, Wiltshire

For Dawn (Bur)

Page 2 (recto) of Leibniz's handwritten manuscript LH 37, 4ff 14r–15v

Contents

Acknowledgements

I would like to thank Philip Beeley, Jonathan Bennett, Dan Cook, Harry Parkinson, Michael Pickles, Hartmut Rudolph, John Thorley, Elizabeth Vinestock and Geert de Wilde for looking over my translations and making suggestions that greatly improved the end result. I would also like to thank Dan Cook and Vernon Pratt for looking over the introductory essay.

Selected Bibliography

1. Original language editions. The abbreviations on the left are used throughout this volume as shorthand references.

D *Opera Omnia* (ed. L. Dutens), 6 volumes, Geneva, 1768.

C *Opuscles et fragments inédits de Leibniz* (ed. Louis Couturat), Paris: Félix Alcan, 1903.

G *Die philosophischen Schriften von Gottfried Wilhelm Leibniz* (ed. C. I. Gerhardt), 7 volumes, Berlin: Weidmann, 1875–90.

FC *Lettres et opuscules inédits de Leibniz* (ed. Louis Alexandre Foucher de Careil), Paris: Ladrange, 1854.

GM *Mathematische Schriften* (ed. C. I. Gerhardt), 7 volumes, Berlin: A. Asher, 1849–63.

E *Opera Philosophica* (ed. J. E. Erdmann), Berlin: Eichler, 1839–40.

A *Sämtliche schriften und briefe* (ed. Akademie der Wissenschaften), multiple volumes in 6 series, Berlin: Akademie Verlag, 1923–.

Gr *Textes inédits* (ed. Gaston Grua), 2 volumes with successive pagination, Paris: Presses Universitaires de France, 1948.

K *Correspondenz von Leibniz mit der Prinzessin Sophie*, 3 volumes, Hildesheim: Georg Olms, 1973.

VE *Vorausedition zur Reihe IV band VI in der Ausgabe des Akademie der Wissenschaften* (ed. Leibniz Edition, Potsdam), 2005.

2. English editions

DSR *De summa rerum* (trans. and ed. G. H. R. Parkinson), New Haven: Yale University Press, 1992.

LC *The Labyrinth of the Continuum* (trans. and ed. Richard T. W. Arthur), New Haven: Yale University Press, 2001.

The Leibniz–Arnauld Correspondence (trans. and ed. H. T. Mason), Manchester: Manchester University Press, 1967.

Leibniz Selections (trans. and ed. P. Wiener), New York: Scribner, 1951.

Leibniz's 'New System' and associated Contemporary Texts (trans. and ed. R. S. Woolhouse and Richard Francks), Oxford: Clarendon Press, 1997.

Logical Papers (trans. and ed. G. H. R. Parkinson), Oxford: Oxford University Press, 1966.

Monadology and other Philosophical Essays (trans. and ed. Paul Schrecker and Anne Martin Schrecker), Indianapolis: Bobbs-Merrill, 1965.

New Essays concerning Human Understanding (trans. and ed. Peter Remnant and Jonathan Bennett), Cambridge: Cambridge University Press, 1996.

Philosophical Essays (trans. and ed. Roger Ariew and Daniel Garber), Indianapolis: Hackett, 1989.

L *Philosophical Papers and Letters* (trans. and ed. Leroy E. Loemker), Dordrecht: D. Reidel, 1969 (2nd edition).

Philosophical Writings (trans. and ed. G. H. R. Parkinson and Mary Morris), London: Dent, 1973.

Political Writings (trans. and ed. Patrick Riley), Cambridge: Cambridge University Press, 1972.

H *Theodicy* (trans. E. M. Huggard, ed. A. Farrar), Chicago: Open Court, 1990.

Writings on China (trans. and ed. Daniel J. Cook and Henry Rosemont Jr.), Chicago: Open Court, 1994.

Select bibliography of works on Leibniz (in English)

Adam, Robert Merrihew. *Leibniz: Determinist, Theist, Idealist,* Oxford: Oxford University Press, 1994.

Broad, C. D. *Leibniz,* Cambridge: Cambridge University Press, 1975.

Brown, Stuart. *Leibniz,* Brighton: Harvester Press, 1984.

Brown, Stuart and Fox, N. J. *The Historical Dictionary of Leibniz's Philosophy,* Oxford: Scarecrow Press, 2006.

Hooker, Michael (ed.). *Leibniz: Critical and Interpretive Essays,* Manchester: Manchester University Press, 1982.

Jolley, Nicholas (ed.). *The Cambridge Companion to Leibniz,* Cambridge: Cambridge University Press, 1995.

Jolley, Nicholas. *Leibniz,* London: Routledge, 2005.

Mercer, Christia. *Leibniz's Metaphysics*, Cambridge: Cambridge University Press, 2001.

Rescher, Nicholas. *Leibniz's Metaphysics of Nature*, Dordrecht: D. Reidel, 1981.

Riley, Patrick. *Leibniz' Universal Jurisprudence*, Cambridge, Massachusetts: Harvard University Press, 1996.

Ross, George MacDonald. *Leibniz*, Oxford: Oxford University Press, 1984.

Russell, Bertrand. *The Philosophy of Leibniz*, London: Routledge, 1937 (2nd edition).

Rutherford, Donald. *Leibniz and the Rational Order of Nature*, Cambridge: Cambridge University Press, 1995.

Strickland, Lloyd. *Leibniz Reinterpreted*, London: Continuum, 2006.

Wilson, Catherine. *Leibniz's Metaphysics*, Manchester: Manchester University Press, 1989.

Woolhouse, Roger. *Descartes, Spinoza, Leibniz*, Routledge: London, 1993.

Other historical source

ACW Aristotle 1984, *The Complete Works of Aristotle* (trans. Jonathan Barnes), New Jersey: Princeton University Press.

Introduction

There were many geniuses in that extraordinary age straddling the seventeenth and eighteenth centuries when Europe was on the cusp of the Enlightenment, but perhaps none so deserving of the name than Gottfried Wilhelm Leibniz. Born in Leipzig on 1 July 1646, Leibniz was the son of a professor of moral philosophy at Leipzig University. If his later recollections can be believed, he taught himself Latin at an early age in order to read the books in his father's library. He obtained the degree of Bachelor of Philosophy from the University of Leipzig at the age of 17, and a doctorate in Laws from the University of Altdorf at the age of 20. Following the award of his doctorate, Leibniz was offered a professorship at the University of Jena, which he turned down, choosing instead to accept a post working for the Elector of Mainz. In 1672 he was sent to Paris on a diplomatic mission to persuade the emperor of France to invade Egypt rather than Germany. Whilst in Paris Leibniz met Antoine Arnauld and Nicolas Malebranche, two of Europe's greatest philosophers at the time, and mathematician-physicist Christiaan Huygens. Three years into his stay in Paris, Leibniz discovered the infinitesimal calculus, though this was not published until 1684.

In late 1676 Leibniz accepted a post as Court Councillor at Hanover, which brought his time in France to an end. Leibniz's route back to Germany was not a straightforward one, however, and involved stops in England and Holland. Whilst in Holland he met Spinoza, already well known as a philosopher, and Antony van Leeuwenhoek, one of the first microscopists. In Hanover Leibniz's duties were various, and included librarian, political advisor, technical consultant and, much later, unofficial diplomat. In 1686 he was given the duty of writing a history of the House of Brunswick. Although Leibniz lived for another thirty years, he never completed this history and spent much of his time with projects that were clearly much closer to his heart. In 1682 he assisted in the founding of the journal *Acta Eruditorum*, in which he published a number of important papers. He expended a great deal of effort attempting to facilitate a reunion between the Catholic and Protestant churches. He lobbied tirelessly for the foundation of scientific academies, and was eventually rewarded for his efforts with the setting up of one such academy in Berlin in 1700 (of which Leibniz was made president). He created calculating machines, drew up plans for the development of a universal encyclopaedia that would contain everything that was so far known, wrote Latin poetry, funded alchemical research, and undertook studies on the origin of languages. But such projects by no means exhausted Leibniz's interests – during his life he made original contributions to physics, mathematics, logic, geology, law, politics, economics, linguistics, and of course philosophy. Much of Leibniz's philosophy was developed in his spare time, through short papers written for himself, book notes, and hasty jottings. In the seventeenth and eighteenth centuries it was common for thinkers to communicate their ideas to others via letters, which were often copied and distributed to other scholars or even published, and Leibniz often disseminated his philosophical ideas this way. During his life he counted among his correspondents many of the finest minds of Europe – as well as Malebranche and Arnauld, Leibniz had fruitful exchanges with heavyweight thinkers such as Christian Wolff, Pierre Bayle, Bernard le Bovier de Fontenelle and Samuel Clarke, as well as with interested amateurs such as the Electress Sophie of Hanover and her daughter, Queen Sophie Charlotte of Prussia. Leibniz also published some of his ideas in the handful of scholarly journals that existed in his day. By and large this piecemeal approach to the diffusion of his ideas suited Leibniz just fine; by his own confession, he did not have the inclination to write a lengthy treatise that brought all the parts of his philosophical system together. His two longest philosophical works – the *New Essays on Human Understanding* (written 1703–4 though not published until 1749) and the *Theodicy* (1710) were by no means straightforward expositions of his system, but rather detailed responses to the work of John Locke and Pierre Bayle respectively. Despite only drip-feeding various parts of his philosophy to the public via letters and short journal articles, by the end of the seventeenth century Leibniz had established his reputation as a philosopher, though it would be fair to say that his standing as a mathematician and logician was far higher, at least as far as many of his contemporaries was concerned. (Leibniz published but a tiny fraction of his philosophical writings during his lifetime, and it has only been through the posthumous publication of his private papers – a process that continues today – that the breadth and depth of his philosophical thinking has become apparent.) Leibniz's last years were mostly spent working on the never-to-be-completed history of the House of Brunswick, and attempting to popularize his philosophical views through papers circulated to well-placed acquaintances and 'popular' writings for the educated public (the *Theodicy* was very much part of this attempt). Leibniz's eventful life finally came to an end in Hanover on 14 November 1716.

Metaphysics

Arguably, the doctrine for which Leibniz is today most famous (or infamous) is that of optimism, that is, his claim that the existing world is the best of all possible worlds. For Leibniz, a possible thing was one that did not imply a contradiction, and much like contemporary modal logicians he envisaged all the things that satisfied this definition as forming different sets: 'There are as many series of things that can be imagined not involving contradiction as there are possible worlds . . . for I call "possible" that which does not imply contradiction' (Gr 390). The reason why Leibniz thought that there were various possible worlds rather than one giant possible world that contained every single possible thing was because he thought that not all possibles were *compossible*. That is, some possibles were not compatible with each other, and thus were not jointly realizable. So a possible world was not merely a collection of possibles, but a collection of *com*possibles: 'there are many possible universes, each collection of compossibles making up one of them' (L 662).

Leibniz often claimed that every possible thing had within it 'a certain demand for existence or . . . a claim to exist' (p. 32 below), and thus would exist unless something else prevented it. Although the idea of possibles 'striving for existence' is an intriguing one, it was in fact little more than a figurative device to refer to God's criteria of selection for existence. For as Leibniz conceded, 'possible things have no existence at all and therefore have no power to make themselves exist' (A VI iv 2232), so they could not strictly speaking strive, strain or struggle for existence at all. Yet although possible things had no actual existence, Leibniz argued that they were not merely figments of logicians' imagination either, but were ideas or essences that actually subsisted in the mind of God. The 'demands' or 'claims' to existence which Leibniz attributed to each possible thing were in fact nothing more than the degrees of perfection that each thing had, a more perfect thing having more 'claim' or 'right' to exist than a less perfect thing. Thus the set of things with the greatest claim for existence was in fact the most perfect set of all those possible, and the 'striving' of these possible sets was little more than a process whereby God weighed them against each other to determine their relative merit or worthiness for existence. Leibniz held that God's own supreme perfection would make him want to choose the most perfect set of things that he could, and so the end result of this evaluation process is that God chooses the most perfect set of things – the best of all possible worlds. But which set is the best one possible? Leibniz claimed that it is the set containing 'as many things as possible' (p. 30), or the set in 'which most things co-exist' (p. 195). But as many of *what*, exactly? The answer is *substances*.

In seventeenth-century metaphysics the notion of substance was of the utmost importance since the search for substance was in fact the search for what was constitutive of reality, i.e. the ultimate stuff or stuffs out of which reality was composed. One of the most popular views on substance in Leibniz's day was that put forward by René Descartes (1596–1650), who argued that there were two kinds of substance, i.e. basic constituents of the world: material substance (body) and mental substance (mind, or soul), the first kind characterized by extension, i.e. the filling up of space, the second by thought, i.e. consciousness. Although this dualism of substances was endorsed by many of the leading lights of the late seventeenth century, it found no favour with Leibniz, who until the mid-1690s or thereabouts preferred the Aristotelian/Scholastic view that a substance was a composite of matter (the stuff out of which a thing is made) and substantial form (the specific shape, arrangement or structure of matter, or in more complex cases its *function*). However around the mid-1690s Leibniz developed his own account of substance, which held that a substance was an immaterial soul or soul-like being. Curiously enough, Leibniz's various definitions of substance seemed to have remained relatively stable over time, despite there being a shift in his thinking as to what actually satisfied these definitions. For instance, he claimed that a substance is

an ultimate subject of predicates, possessing a concept that is complete (see pp. 42–3)
a unity (see p. 53)

the source of actions (see p. 73)

Although these characterizations initially led Leibniz to the view that a substance was a composite of matter and form, in what follows I shall focus on their role in his later view that a substance was an immaterial soul or soul-like being.

By characterizing substance in the ways noted above, Leibniz placed himself squarely within the Aristotelian tradition that had dominated philosophy prior to Descartes. In the fourth century BC Aristotle had defined a substance as an ultimate subject of predicates (ACW 1017b23), and also a subject that underwent change (ACW 4a18–19). By the Middle Ages Aristotle's characterization of substance had become the conventional wisdom, and by the seventeenth century was part of the Scholastic tradition that was widely taught and accepted throughout Europe. To Aristotle's own characterization of substance, post-Aristotelian thinkers had added the stipulation that a substance also be a unity. It is with this that I shall begin my account of Leibnizian substance.

The requirement that a substance be a unity was an inevitable corollary of what a substance was supposed to be, namely an ultimate constituent of the world. As Leibniz realized, and as did the Scholastics before him, if a thing was divisible then it would not be something truly basic, an ultimate constituent of the world. A substance thus had to be a simple thing, that is, a thing without parts, and hence truly a single being – a unity. Leibniz eventually adopted the term 'monad' to refer to such unities, the word deriving from 'monas', the Greek word for unity, or that which is one.

As Leibniz saw it, because a substance was something without parts and thus indivisible, that ruled out matter as a plausible candidate, since matter 'is only a collection or mass of parts to infinity' (p. 69). That is, any material thing can be divided and divided again, and so on, there being no reason, according to Leibniz, why this process of division should ever come to a halt. Thus a substance could not be some kind of ultimate physical point, a hard indivisible atom of matter, and consequently it had to be some kind of non-physical point, or what Leibniz sometimes referred to as a 'metaphysical point' (p. 73). Perhaps unsurprisingly, Leibniz often referred to these substances as 'souls' (or 'soul-like' entities), which seems an appropriate description given their status as non-physical unities.

Following Aristotle and the Scholastic tradition, Leibniz also claimed that a substance was an ultimate subject of predicates, that is, a subject of predicates which was not itself a predicate of anything else. So, for instance, Plato would qualify as a substance as Plato could not be predicated of anything else, i.e. he can exist in his own right, whereas a bruise would not qualify as a substance because it can be predicated of other things, for example Plato (in the proposition 'Plato has a bruise'). In characterizing the notion of substance in this way, Leibniz was not simply attempting to re-establish the Aristotelian/Scholastic notion that had been largely swept aside by Descartes' dualism, but to develop it. For as I have already noted, Leibniz claimed that a substance was not just an ultimate subject of predicates, but also possessed a concept that contained *all* the predicates that would ever belong to it:

> The complete or perfect concept of an individual substance contains all of its predicates, past, present and future. For certainly it is true now that a future predicate is future, and so is contained in the concept of the thing. And hence all the things that will happen to Peter or Judas, both necessary and free, are contained in the perfect individual concept of Peter or Judas (p. 50).

Why, though, did Leibniz insist that substances had to have concepts containing all of their predicates, rather than just be subjects of predicates, as Aristotle believed? The answer Leibniz appears to offer is that the complete concept theory of substance is a straightforward consequence of his theory of truth. The nature of truth demands, he argued, that in all true propositions 'the concept of the predicate is always in some way included in that of the subject' (p. 47). To give a simple example, in the true proposition 'a mortal man is mortal' the concept of the predicate 'mortal' is clearly included in the concept of the subject 'a mortal man', and that explains why the proposition is true. And Leibniz believed that *all* true propositions were ultimately of this form, though most were not obviously so clear cut as the example just given. For example, Leibniz would argue that the true proposition 'Plato wrote the *Republic*' is true by virtue of the fact that the concept of the predicate 'wrote the *Republic*' is included in or belongs to the concept of 'Plato', even though we cannot demonstrate this. However Leibniz's view was that a thorough unpacking of the concept of 'Plato' would reveal that the predicate 'wrote the *Republic*' was indeed included in it, or belonged to it, although in this case – and many others – the unpacking could only be done by God, who alone grasps the complete concept of every subject. But in any case, for Leibniz all truths are ultimately reducible to identities, i.e. tautologies like 'a mortal man is a man', even if it is beyond human powers to see this reduction through to the very end in most cases. This conception of truth provided the foundation for one of Leibniz's most famous principles, the principle of sufficient reason, 'the common axiom that nothing happens without a reason, and that one can always explain why a thing turned out thus rather than otherwise' (p. 47). What the principle of sufficient reason says, in effect, is that there is always a reason why a true proposition is true, the reason of course being, in Leibniz's view, that in true propositions the concept of the predicate is contained in the concept of the subject (think of the proposition 'a mortal man is mortal' described above, and how the fact that the predicate belongs to the subject explains why the proposition is true). Thus it was because of this theory of truth that Leibniz claimed a substance was not merely a subject of predicates, as Aristotle had claimed, but of *all* the predicates that could truly be ascribed to it; namely because the concept of whatever can be truly predicated of a substance must already be contained in the concept of that substance in order for it to be truly predicated at all. The concepts of substances must therefore be complete.

A consequence of the 'complete concept' theory of substance that Leibniz was often keen to draw was that every single substance had to contain within itself a 'representation' or 'reflection' of everything else in the universe. For if the concept of every substance was complete, then it would have to contain predicates that spell out in complete detail the various relations of that substance to all the other things outside of it. And of course when any of these other things happened to change, these changes would have to be reflected in that substance, its predicates changing to keep up with what was going on outside of it. So with Leibnizian substances, 'when a change occurs in one, there follows some corresponding change in all the others' (p. 51), and consequently the states of one 'mirror' or 'reflect' the states of all the others.

Substances, then, are unities, and subjects of all the predicates that will ever belong to them (and thus 'mirrors' of every other substance in the universe). As I noted earlier, in addition to those things, Leibniz also thought that a substance was the source of actions, or rather, its own actions. One reason Leibniz offered for this view was that it was impossible to conceive how one immaterial substance could have an effect on another. The fact that substances could not be acted upon by any other substance entailed that substances were 'a world apart', as Leibniz sometimes put it, i.e. completely independent of each other, at least causally. Given that, the principle behind each substance's changes of state could either lie in the substances themselves, or in God. Leibniz was generally averse to invoking a *Deus ex machina* explanation for everyday occurrences like change, which left him with the option that each substance brings about its own changes of state, a view which, as we have seen, he was happy to embrace (and it was on account of this view that Leibniz sometimes referred to substances as 'entelechies', an entelechy being Aristotle's word for a source or principle of action). Substances, then, bring about their own changes from one state to another, and they do this, Leibniz thought, in accordance with their own individual concepts. Thus the complete concept possessed by every substance ultimately functioned as a sort of blueprint or script for a substance's own changes, dictating what its state should be and when.

For Leibniz, the ultimate constituents of reality are therefore substances/souls/monads/unities, which are simple and indivisible, and the sources of their own actions. And so far as Leibniz was concerned, that was all there was in the world: 'I believe that there are only monads in nature, everything else being only phenomena that result from them' (p. 54). The question raised by this, obviously, is how do simple, metaphysical points, that have no spatial properties at all, give rise to the extended, physical things of the world as we know it? Leibniz's answer is this: 'matter is not composed of constitutive unities, but results from them' (p. 130). But what does he mean when he says that matter 'results from' substances? The answer lies in what Leibniz thought substances ultimately were: in Leibniz's view, although substances were simple and indivisible, they nevertheless contained two 'principles' or features, which Leibniz described variously as 'positive and privative, perfection and imperfection, value and limits, active and passive, form (i.e. entelechy, endeavour, energy) and matter or mass' (p. 39). The first thing to note is that each pair of opposites on this list is intended to be equivalent to the others, so that 'positive', 'perfection', 'value', etc., mean the same thing, likewise 'privative', 'imperfection', 'limits', etc. In other words, then, every single substance has some degree of perfection, value and so on, and some degree of imperfection, limits and so on, though these vary from substance to substance (and from the fact that every substance has some perfection it becomes clear why Leibniz thought the best world would contain as many of them as possible). In fact Leibniz envisaged created substances as forming a sort of hierarchy, book-ended by God, who is pure positive/perfection/value/activity, etc., and pure nothingness, which is literally nothing.

Now the interesting thing about Leibniz's list of the principles that make up each created substance is that it includes matter, which he identifies with a substance's privative or passive aspect. Elsewhere, Leibniz calls this passive aspect either the substance's 'primary matter', or its 'primitive passive force' (the positive/active aspect of substances being the 'primitive active force'; the figure opposite may help to illustrate Leibniz's claim that each substance has two sides or aspects). Now strictly speaking, this primary matter is not matter as physicists understand it, but merely the extent to which a substance is imperfect, limited, etc. (i.e. the extent to which it falls short of God). The reason Leibniz gives for why this primary matter cannot be the subject of physics is because physics deals with aggregates or composite things, whereas primary matter is in itself 'something incomplete' (p. 126), being only the passive part of a substance. However Leibniz holds that when many substances are grouped together, the aggregation of their passive sides, their primary matter, gives rise to 'secondary matter', which *is* the stuff of physical things in the world of experience. But of course secondary matter is not literally composed from substances' primary matter, because primary matter – being merely the passive part of an immaterial substance – has no dimensions or extension at all, so an aggregation of primary matter will not have dimensions or extension either. Yet according to Leibniz, when other substances *perceive* such an aggregation of primary matter, they perceive it as secondary matter, i.e. body. In other words, groupings of primary matter *manifest themselves* as solid, material objects to perceiving subjects. The matter of our day-to-day experience is thus a phenomenon, in the sense that it is an object of perception and nothing more, which means that it has

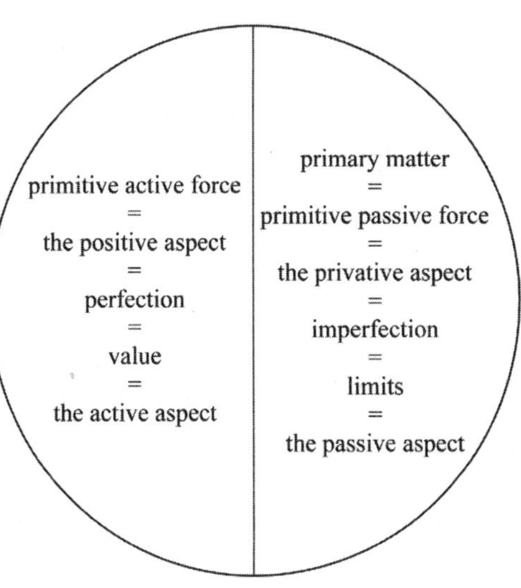

The make up of a Leibnizian substance

reality only insofar as substances perceive it to have reality. But it is what Leibniz calls a 'well-ordered and exact phenomenon' (p. 54), in that its properties are grounded in the properties of the substances that give rise to it. Strictly speaking, then, matter is not *composed* from the passive elements of various substances, but *derives* from them: 'there are infinite simple substances or creatures in any particle of matter, and matter is composed from them, not as from parts, but as from constitutive principles' (p. 53). Thus all physical things are composed (in the Leibnizian sense just explained) of substances; the bodies of humans and animals are too, but with those, Leibniz argues, there is a dominant substance, which is the soul of the human or animal, and an infinity of other substances that make up its body.

Mind, body and soul

One corollary of Leibniz's decision to populate the world with simple substances and only simple substances was that he felt able to draw the conclusion that the world ultimately contained things that could not be destroyed. Like many of his time, Leibniz accepted ancient Greek thinking that 'every natural destruction consists in the dissolution of parts' (p. 64), and as all created things were unities and hence had no parts that could be subject to dissolution, they could not therefore be destroyed. Consequently, once a substance had been created, it would continue to exist unless it was literally annihilated by a special act of God, something Leibniz thought was unlikely to happen given God's perfect goodness. This meant that in Leibniz's philosophy it was not only the substances corresponding to human souls that were indestructible, but also the substances corresponding to *all* souls, including animal ones. Leibniz attempted to sidestep the potential theological problems involved with the suggestion that animal souls are as durable as human souls by drawing a sharp distinction between the types of soul that they were. Human souls, he argued, were true *minds*, in that they possessed the faculty of reason, whereas animal souls were not true minds because they were not rational. What this ultimately meant was that humans would retain their personality, for 'as the rational soul possesses reflection, which is to say that it presently thinks of itself and knows itself, it is appropriate that it should always know itself' (p. 84). The ordinary souls of animals, however, have no capacity for self-knowledge, and so even though they are indestructible they nevertheless do not enjoy immortality proper, as immortality requires the preservation of the individual personality or self.

Leibniz's division of substances into rational souls and ordinary souls not only enabled him to sidestep the charge that he granted animals the same immortality as humans, but also provided an answer to a question much-discussed in Leibniz's day, namely how a person could be sure that *her* soul would be immortal. The worry was that, if a person's existence is interrupted by death, then her soul would have to be recreated by God at a later date, and the fact that it would be recreated made it difficult to know if what was being recreated was truly the original soul, or just a frighteningly accurate copy of it. In Leibniz's view, there was no death to interrupt the continued existence of each individual, and as all rational souls would 'retain sensation and consciousness' (p. 67) they would thus never lose the 'moral qualities of their personality' (p. 72) and hence for them continued existence would be true immortality – the survival of their personality.

Another of the key philosophical problems in the late seventeenth century concerned how mind and body 'communicate', or interact. The problem stemmed from Descartes' belief that mind and body were separate substances; given that mind is a spiritual substance with no physical properties at all, and that body was a physical substance with no spiritual properties, how, it was commonly asked, could one have any effect on the other? Descartes had notoriously argued that the mind could in fact have an effect on the body, and vice versa, with this occurring in the brain's pineal gland. So when a person decided to waggle their toes, for instance, their non-physical mind or soul somehow influenced their physical pineal gland, which in turn sent the required signals down to the toes for waggling to occur. Such was Descartes' view. Although Descartes' philosophy had a great many supporters in the seventeenth century, very few of them felt able to accept his theory that mind and body exercised direct influence on each other. And so the problem of how these two different kinds of substances interacted, as they seemed to do, was an acute one.

Strictly speaking, the problem of the communication of substances, if we might call it that, was not one that obviously arose in Leibniz's system. As we have already seen, Leibniz rejected Descartes' view that mind and body were two kinds of substance. In so doing, he rejected the very framework in which the problem of the communication of substances arose. Nevertheless, Leibniz often wrote as if he did accept this framework, and therefore as if the problem of how substances communicated *did* concern him as much as would anyone else who accepted the same framework. His own solution to the problem of the communication of substances, namely the pre-established harmony (or the 'hypothesis of concomitance' as he called it in earlier writings), thus often made it seem as if Leibniz was in fact a closet Cartesian when in fact he was not. In any case, the solution Leibniz put forward was this: although there is no interaction at all between mind and body, it *looks like* there is because God so established things from the very beginning that although minds and bodies follow their own laws, their states nevertheless harmonize. That is, at the exact time that physical laws cause damage to my leg, the psychical laws (i.e. the laws that apply to minds) bring it about that my mind feels the pain, *just as if the damage to my leg had actually caused it.* Thus with regard to soul and body, Leibniz argued that 'each of these substances . . . by only following its own laws which it received with its being . . . nevertheless agrees with the other, just as if there were a mutual influence' (pp. 77–8). But properly speaking, of course, for Leibniz the true pre-established harmony was not one that held between mind and body as such, but between all *individual substances*: 'monads agree between themselves, being mirrors of the same universe to infinity . . . [i]t is in this that consists my pre-established harmony' (p. 54). In other words, God had established not so much a harmony between soul and body, but a harmony between the states of every single substance in the entire universe, each accurately mirroring all the others' changing states. Hence 'different substances of the same system of the world are created from the beginning in such a way that from the laws of their own nature they harmonize with one another' (p. 68).

Free will and necessity

A common objection raised against the pre-established harmony was that if substances had been pre-arranged from the beginning, as Leibniz suggested, so that their states always agreed despite there being no causal interaction between them, then everything that will ever happen to every substance will have been determined right from the beginning of things. Leibniz was well aware that complete determination was a consequence of his pre-established harmony, and was not fazed by it at all, happily granting that, in the world, 'everything is absolutely certain and *determined*' (p. 96). His detractors, however, urged that if this was indeed the case, then there could be no free will. In Leibniz's day, the most widely accepted notion of free will was a *freedom of indifference* (today often called *libertarian* free will), according to which an action is free if and only if it has not been in any way determined beforehand. And according to Leibniz's critics, it was this very notion of freedom that seemed impossible to square with the system of pre-established harmony. With this assessment Leibniz agreed, and he made no attempt at all to make room in his system for this freedom of indifference. Leibniz was not complacent about the issue of free will, however, but the problem, as he saw it, was that philosophers had employed entirely the wrong conception of it. He denounced the freedom of indifference as a 'chimera', on the grounds that it supposed that actions could occur literally without any reasons or causes at all – a clear violation of the principle of sufficient reason. As he put it, 'there is always a reason that inclines us towards one action rather than another, since nothing happens without a reason' (p. 94). But if there is a reason for everything we do, how do we know which of our actions are free? Leibniz's answer is that we act freely when the reason (or determination) for our action comes from ourselves rather than from anything outside of us. And conversely, an act is unfree when the reason (or determination) comes from outside of us. To use Leibniz's own examples, 'if someone is pulled into a house by force then it cannot be said that he went there freely', because the determination for the action lies not in the person who did the action, but in the one pulling him. Whereas, claimed Leibniz, 'those who are caught at sea during a storm [and] throw their goods overboard in order to make the ship lighter and to save themselves' *do* act freely, 'because they are not forced to save themselves if they do not want to do so' (pp. 91–2). The desire to save oneself is the determination for the latter action, and as this determination comes from inside the agent the resulting action is for Leibniz a free one. In both cases Leibniz was happy to concede that the actions were fully determined in advance, but he also stressed that this was entirely irrelevant for the purpose of deciding whether they were free or not; for that, the relevant factor was whether the determination for the action came from inside the agent, in which case the action was free, or outside the agent, in which case it was unfree. Considered in this way, Leibniz argued, free will is entirely compatible with determinism (a feature that led to the concept of free will advocated by Leibniz being termed *compatibilism*, though this was not a term that had been coined in Leibniz's day).

It would be fair to say that Leibniz's doctrine of free will has often been seen as problematic. Whatever merits it may have in itself, it seems hard to square with some of Leibniz's metaphysical commitments. For as we know, in the Leibnizian universe there are only simple, immaterial substances which do not causally interact with each other, each instead being the source of its own changes which it brings about in accordance with its own complete concept. As such, every action of every substance would seem to satisfy Leibniz's criterion for being a free action, including those actions that substances did not 'will' to do. But Leibniz's doctrine of substance appears to give rise to an even more serious problem, which is this: because every true proposition about a substance is true by virtue of the fact that the concept of a substance's predicates are already contained in the concept of that substance, every true proposition about that substance would appear to be a necessary truth. The problem becomes obvious when we recall Leibniz's belief that all truths are either identities (tautologies) like 'a mortal man is mortal', or are ultimately reducible to them, because such truths are generally thought to be necessary. A necessary truth is usually defined as one that could not possibly be false, or as Leibniz defines it, one 'whose opposite . . . is impossible or implies a contradiction' (p. 95). Now 'a mortal man is mortal' is obviously a necessary truth, because its opposite is impossible (and does imply a contradiction), and from that one example it is easy to see why it is widely believed that all such identities are necessary truths. But it also seems that truths which are reducible to identities, such as 'a bachelor is an unmarried man' are also necessary. In this example, by substituting the definition of 'bachelor' for the term 'bachelor', the proposition becomes 'an unmarried man is an unmarried man' – an identity and a necessary truth. But it seems just as impossible to deny that 'a bachelor is an unmarried man' as it is to deny that 'a bachelor is a bachelor', as in either case the denial involves a clear contradiction. Thus it would seem that the truths that are ultimately reducible to identities are no less necessary than the identities that they are reducible to. But these are the only sorts of truths that Leibniz recognizes, and if they are all necessary then obviously there can be no contingency in the Leibnizian universe at all.

It must be said that Leibniz took this charge very seriously, and one way in which he proposed to escape it was by drawing this distinction: with necessary truths, he argued, it could be demonstrated that the predicate is contained in the subject in a finite number of steps, and so necessary truths were either explicitly identities, like 'a mortal man is mortal', or those that could be demonstrated to be reducible to such identities by a finite analysis. However with contingent truths, Leibniz argued, it would require an infinity of steps to demonstrate that the predicate is contained in the subject, which meant that for practical purposes the inclusion of the predicate in the subject was not something that could be demonstrated at all:

> in necessary propositions, when the analysis is continued for a time, we arrive at an identical equation . . . In contingent propositions, however, the analysis continues to infinity through reasons of reasons, so that we never have a full demonstration, although there is always an underlying reason for the truth, even if it is only perfectly understood by God, who alone penetrates an infinite series in one stroke of the mind (p. 111).

To illustrate Leibniz's point, consider again the proposition 'a bachelor is an unmarried man'. As we have seen, reducing this to an identical proposition requires just one step of analysis, namely replacing the term 'bachelor' with its definition ('unmarried man'). As such, 'a bachelor is an unmarried man' qualifies as a necessary truth for Leibniz. Now consider a proposition Leibniz would consider to be contingent, such as 'Leibniz claimed that all matter resulted from the primitive passive forces of substances'. Although Leibniz would agree that the predicate 'claimed that all matter resulted from the primitive passive forces of substances' was one that belonged to his complete concept, he would deny that this could be demonstrated in a finite number of steps, given the infinite complexity of the world and of all the things in it. And as such, Leibniz would claim it to be a contingent truth rather than a necessary one.

Science

Whether it is a contingent truth about Leibniz or not, he *did* explain matter as resulting from the primitive passive forces of substances, as I have already noted. This was by no means a common analysis of what matter was, and in order to give credence to his own account of matter Leibniz attempted to show that rival accounts were inadequate. The most widely accepted account of matter in Leibniz's day was that given by Descartes, namely that the essence of matter consisted in extension alone, that is, in something that takes up space. Against this, Leibniz argued that if matter were nothing more than extension, a moving body colliding with a body at rest would result in both bodies moving away with the same speed and direction of the body that was initially in motion (see p. 125). But this was not what happened in real-life cases, in which moving bodies invariably slowed down when hitting other bodies at rest, and sometimes even rebounded from them. To Leibniz this demonstrated that there must be more to matter than mere extension; specifically it suggested to him that matter must also possess *resistance*, that is, the ability to resist change. This property, he believed, was not one that could be derived from mere extension, which led him to claim that the Cartesian conception of matter was wrong, or rather incomplete, and required one to invoke *force* (from which, he believed, resistance *could* be derived) alongside extension as comprising the true essence of matter.

Another hypothesis in vogue among the physicists of Leibniz's day was that of atomism. Introduced by Pierre Gassendi,[1] and defended by Gérauld de Cordemoy and Robert Boyle amongst others, this hypothesis held that the whole of nature was ultimately composed of tiny unsplittable bits of matter called atoms. This was a view that, by Leibniz's own admission, he had flirted with during his youth, before becoming dissatisfied with it. Much of this dissatisfaction had to do with atomism's central claim that if a chunk of matter were to be continually divided a bit would eventually be reached that could not be further divided. Leibniz found this very difficult to grasp, for in his view 'no reason can be given why bodies of a certain smallness should not be further divisible' (p. 52). Leibniz thus construed the atomists as meaning that the indivisible part of matter – the atom – was in fact made up of smaller parts of matter that were inseparably connected (and so resistant to further division) only by some kind of insuperable attachment. Leibniz found such an idea wholly unsatisfactory as he could ascertain no natural reason for such an attachment, and this led him to suppose that if God had created atoms then he would have to keep their parts together 'by a perpetual miracle'. But if that was how atoms came to be indivisible, 'then they will not be natural atoms, or rather they will be atoms which are indivisible by a certain occult quality lodged in them' (G III 506). And this he found bizarre and 'contrary to reason' (p. 73), and thus wholly unbecoming of a perfectly wise creator.

It can be said with some fairness that Leibniz was generally dissatisfied with most of the prevailing views in the physics of his day. His chief gripe was that most physical hypotheses overlooked one important fact: 'the general principles of physics and even of mechanics depend on the conduct of a sovereign intelligence, and cannot be explained without taking it into consideration' (p. 134). The fact that everything had been created and ordered by God, the wisest of possible beings, had far-reaching consequences in Leibniz's view. Aside from the ruling-out of atoms, a good example of such a consequence is Leibniz's belief that all change in the universe came about in accordance with what he called *the law of continuity*, which he often summed up by saying that 'there is no change *by a leap*' (p. 137). What Leibniz meant by this was that, wherever change occurred in the universe, it always occurred smoothly via all intermediate points or steps, so that there were no gaps or discontinuities. Leibniz did not envisage the law of continuity as a true law of physics, on a par with the laws of motion, but rather as the metaphysical underpinning of all such physical laws. In other words, the law of continuity was a higher order law or principle 'written in' to the laws of nature that scientists studied. Leibniz held this to be so because physical laws that obeyed the law of continuity produced more elegant results than those that did not, and as such they would have appealed to God on account of their elegance.

But Leibniz's scientific interests were not restricted to physics; he also took a keen interest in what would nowadays be called biology. He was an avowed follower of the theory of preformationism, developed by Leeuwenhoek. As a result of his observations, Leeuwenhoek held that all animals (men included) that were to develop throughout the course of the universe began as spermatic animalcules, that is, miniature versions of the animals they were to become, that were present in the semen of all previous generations of animals. Although Leibniz accepted this view in its entirety, he also drew what he considered to be a natural consequence of it, namely that if an animal 'does not begin naturally, it does not end naturally either; thus death in turn will be nothing other than an involution and diminution of the animal, when it returns from the state of a large animal to the state of an animalcule' (pp. 65–6). Thus death was not true death, merely a change of state – a view that accorded perfectly with Leibniz's belief that there was no destruction in the realm of substances.

Another issue hotly debated among the scientific community of Leibniz's day was that of the origin of fossils. The prevailing view in the late 1600s was that the Earth contained within it, at least in some places, the power to produce rocks featuring the form of an animal, and that fossils were therefore 'tricks of nature'. Leibniz initially endorsed this assessment, claiming that it was 'well known that stones grow and assume a thousand strange forms' (p. 138), though he noted that in some cases the similarity between living creatures and fossil forms was so great as to make it more plausible to suppose that a fossil was in fact the petrified form of a once-living animal. In later discussions on the same subject Leibniz claimed that most fossils were of this type, though he remained unwilling to dismiss the 'tricks of nature' explanation entirely, saying that he would not deny this form of explanation 'in some cases' (p. 143). But stressing the organic origin of (at least some) fossils gave rise to a thorny problem: some of the forms delineated in fossils were of animals and plants that could no longer be found. How was this to be explained? To the modern mind the obvious explanation is that the creatures in question had become extinct, which Leibniz rejected as 'not likely' (p. 139). However he did allow that there might have been what we would today call local extinctions, that is, the extinction of a species from a certain geographical area:

> I even believe that kinds of terrestrial animals that formerly lived on our shores have today perished, whether on account of a climatic change, or on account of other reasons that would be difficult to guess, because of the obscurity of remote matters (p. 143).

It is interesting to note that Leibniz's explanation for local extinctions – climate change – has a strikingly modern ring to it (though Leibniz did not, of course, attribute this change to greenhouse gases!).

Law and ethics

But while some aspects of Leibniz's thinking seem in some way to anticipate modern ideas, others had very deep roots. His views on law are a good case in point, since Leibniz embraced many of the tenets of Roman law which were ancient even in his day, having been introduced by Justinian in the sixth century AD. In accordance with this tradition, Leibniz identified three degrees of right or justice: '*strict right* in commutative justice, *equity* (or charity in the narrower sense of the term) in distributive justice, and finally *piety* (or probity) in universal justice', and from these were derived the three principles of Roman law: 'to injure no one, to give to each his due, and to live honourably (or rather piously)' (p. 150). The aim of the first is to ensure that no one acquires any grounds for a legal claim against us; the aim of the second is 'to benefit all, but only as far as befits each person or as much as each deserves' (p. 150). The motives to follow these precepts may be simple expedience – keeping out of harm's way and being nice to others in the hope that they might reciprocate by being nice to us. But this is not the case with the third precept, to live honourably or piously, which requires one to do good for its own sake. I shall return to this idea shortly.

Leibniz's adherence to Roman ideals is nowhere more apparent than in the practical question of when torture should be employed. In accordance with these ideals, Leibniz was firmly in favour of the use of torture in cases where a person was accused of a very serious crime and the evidence against that person was strong but not strong enough to warrant conviction, at least not safely. In such circumstances, Leibniz urged, the defendant should be subjected to torture in an attempt to extract a confession, which would then allow a court to convict with peace of mind. Not that Leibniz deemed a confession uttered whilst undergoing torture as sufficient – the defendant had to repeat the confession in court, after having been given a little time to recover from his ordeal. And in keeping with Roman tradition, Leibniz argued that if the defendant retracted his confession made under torture, then he should be subjected to torture again. But where Leibniz did differ from Roman law was on the equally practical question of what constituted sufficient grounds for the imposition of capital punishment. Traditional thinking had it that if two witnesses came forward to testify against a defendant who was accused of a very serious crime, and there was no reason to question the integrity of these witnesses, then capital punishment should be imposed, irrespective of whether the defendant admitted the crime or not. Leibniz argued that such a policy was ripe to be abused, 'for what is easier than that two men should conspire to defraud a single person'? (p. 153). Moreover, he argued, 'one may not always be able to distinguish a good man from a crooked man by outward appearance' (p. 153), and consequently it is often difficult to know if a witness is trustworthy or not. Leibniz was not opposed to capital punishment in itself, however; his concern lay rather with the quality of the evidence that was used to impose it, his argument being that much greater evidence was required for crimes meriting the death penalty than those that were dealt with less severely.

While the notion of punishment was very important to Leibniz (in his view, every transgression stood in need of correction by punishment in order to 'satisfy not only the injured party or his family, but also the public, the wise, and wisdom itself' (p. 155), it was not the dominant theme in his ethical thought. Much of that was in fact given over to the perennial questions of how one is to live virtuously, and how one is to obtain happiness. And as Leibniz saw it, these were not two entirely unrelated questions.

First of all, to live virtuously, is, for Leibniz, to live honourably (or piously). As I have briefly mentioned, this involves being minded to procure the common good so far as that is possible. It is tempting to suppose that this means the honourable or pious person will be entirely selfless, and place her own interests below those of others, but Leibniz argues that this is not strictly speaking the case. However such a person will act out of what Leibniz calls 'true love' or 'benevolence' (or sometimes 'generosity'):

> To love is to be delighted by the happiness of someone, or to experience pleasure from the happiness of another. I define this as true love (p. 189).

> *the habit of loving someone is nothing other than* BENEVOLENCE by which we want the good of others, not for the profit that we gain from it, but because it is agreeable to us in itself (p. 170).

To illustrate Leibniz's point, suppose person A did something nice for person B. If A did what she did purely in order to increase B's happiness, which is something A finds pleasing in itself, then A acted out of love or benevolence. But if A did what she did in the hope that it would be reciprocated by B in the future, or in the expectation that she would get some kind of profit from it beyond the pleasure from seeing B happier, then A did *not* act out of love or benevolence. So the motive of an act performed out of true love or benevolence is not entirely selfless, since the act benefits the one who does it as well as the one it was designed to benefit (although it benefits the one who does it only indirectly, since the act first has to benefit someone else and make them happier before the person who performed the act can draw any pleasure from that). To summarize, then, the person who acts out of true love directs her efforts at bringing about an increase in the happiness or well being of others, albeit in the knowledge that she will benefit thereby; and this, in Leibniz's mind, is the mark of true virtue.

Now the fact that an honourable or pious person derives pleasure from acting in the way described means that they are likely to feel joy, which Leibniz claims '*is the total pleasure that results from everything the soul feels at once*' (p. 169). In other words, joy is simply a net balance of pleasure over pain. And if a person succeeds in maintaining this net balance over time then they have attained happiness, which Leibniz defines as 'the state of lasting joy' (p. 164). The link between acting rightly and obtaining happiness is thus clear – by procuring the common good, and so acting out of true love or benevolence, the honourable or pious person secures for herself pleasure, which is the first step on the path to happiness. Moreover, acting out of true love or benevolence 'brings us close to the author of our kind or being, that is to say, to God, insofar as we are capable of imitating him' (p. 159). Thus God serves as the perfect model for the person seeking to live virtuously.

Theology

With God as the lynchpin to so much of his philosophy, it is not surprising that Leibniz expended a great deal of effort in proving God's existence. There were four proofs that he resorted to most frequently, of which two are *a priori* in nature, two *a posteriori*. The first of the *a priori* proofs is a form of what, following Kant, has become known as the ontological argument. In its traditional form, God is defined as the being in which all perfections are contained, and as 'existence' is among the perfections, God must by definition exist. In Leibniz's version of this proof, God is defined as 'being from itself', that is, as a being whose essence involves existence. Leibniz concludes from this definition that God must therefore exist, though he adds the caveat that the proof only works so long as the concept of God is possible, i.e. so long as it does not imply a contradiction. Leibniz's second proof for God's existence is often called the argument from eternal truths. In this argument, Leibniz begins with a necessary truth like 'a circle is the most capacious of isoperimetric shapes' (p. 181), which, he notes, would remain a necessary truth even if there were no circles (or other shapes) in existence, and even if no contingent things existed at all. Consequently it must be the case that this truth about the circle does not depend on any contingent being thinking about it, because it would still remain true even if all contingent beings were eliminated. Therefore this truth, and others like it, cannot be grounded in something contingent. But as necessary truths have a kind of reality they must be grounded in something that exists, and as that something cannot be contingent it must be necessary. This necessary something Leibniz takes to be God, the necessary being. The third proof of God's existence is a form of what Kant was later to call the cosmological argument. In this argument Leibniz takes as his starting point the existence of contingent things. Even though the existence of each contingent thing can be explained by another contingent thing, the series of contingent things taken as a whole is not explained by any contingent thing within that series. 'For a sufficient reason for existence cannot be found in any single thing alone, nor in the whole aggregate and series of things' (p. 31). Therefore in order to find an explanation for the whole series of contingent things, Leibniz argues that we are forced to appeal to something that is outside of the series, and is itself necessary rather than contingent. In other words, the world as a whole can only be explained by positing the existence of God. The fourth proof of God's existence commonly invoked by Leibniz was based on his own theory of pre-established harmony, about which he claimed:

> We also find here a new proof of the existence of God, which is extraordinarily clear. For this perfect agreement of so many substances, which have no communication with one another at all, could come only from a common cause (p. 76).

With God's existence secured on no less than four separate proofs, Leibniz was confident in his assertion that this world must be the best of all those possible. But does the fact that our world is best mean that it has always been as perfect as it could possibly be, or does it actually improve over time (while still remaining better than all rival possible worlds)? To this question Leibniz had no consistent answer. In some texts he argued that the world does *not* get better over time (e.g. p. 196); in others he took the contrary view, that the world *does* undergo improvement (e.g. pp. 39 and 195), while in others written near the end of his life he declared that it was too difficult to come to a decision either way! Throughout these shifts in opinion, however, Leibniz never ceased to believe that the existing world was the best of all those possible.

Perhaps not surprisingly, Leibniz's confidence in the claim that our world is the best one possible has struck many as incredible. Among the most common objections is this one: our world would presumably be better if it contained less evil, and better still if it contained no evil at all, so the presence and quantity of evils in our world strongly suggests that our world is not best. Leibniz's response to this objection was to say that not a single evil could be removed from our world without detriment to the whole: 'We must believe that the mixture of evil has produced the greatest possible good: otherwise the evil would not have been permitted' (p. 208). Elsewhere Leibniz expressed his approval of the Augustinian dictum that 'God would not permit evil unless he could procure a greater good from evil' (p. 197). According to Leibniz, then, evil is prerequisite for a greater good; without the evil, the quantity of good it occasions could not otherwise be realized. But if all evil is indeed bound up with a greater good then one might suppose that this greater good can be demonstrated in at least some instances. But this Leibniz denied:

> For as it is true that there is an infinitely perfect God who has permitted evil, we must say with St. Augustine that he did it for a greater good, although it is beyond the forces of human reason to show *a priori* and in detail in what this good consists. For it is sufficient to know roughly and *a posteriori* that this must be the case, because evil actually happened and God exists (p. 207).

While Leibniz backed away from giving specific instances of where an evil had given rise to a greater good that would not otherwise have come about, he was prepared to say that some evil is permitted by God as punishment for wrongdoing. To be more precise, when someone had perpetrated some evil, and subsequently suffered some misfortune, Leibniz argued that it was right to see a connection between the two apparently separate events and to say that the misfortune was God's punishment for the evil that had been committed (see p. 206). Many cases of sin were, Leibniz believed, punished in this life by some misfortune; moreover, this was not a misfortune brought about by God's miraculous intervention, but through the normal workings of the laws of nature. That is, God had established the world in such a way that sins were often (though not always) naturally followed by misfortunes for those who committed them – a pre-established harmony between certain moral events (sins) and certain natural events (misfortunes) if you will.

But while it was no doubt a fine piece of engineering on God's part to establish this kind of harmony between sins and misfortunes, it does not explain why God should have seen fit to allow sins to occur in the first place. For on the face of it, a world in which no one sins (and in which no punishment is therefore required) would seem to be better than a world of sin and its attendant punishment. So why did God not create such a world? The explanation Leibniz often gave was that sin was in fact an inevitable by-product of the creation process; for as any created beings would fall short of God's absolute perfection, these created beings must of necessity be fallible because they are imperfect: 'We must therefore consider that in all creatures, however excellent they are, there is a certain innate and original limitation or imperfection before every sin, which makes them fallible' (p. 202). Thus not even the best of all possible worlds could be free from creaturely imperfections.

A note on the translations

In preparing this volume I had two aims in mind. First, to introduce Leibniz to those studying him for the first time through the two mediums which he most often used – the short essay or note, and the private letter. Second, to make available to the English-speaking scholar a number of important texts that have not appeared in any previous English anthology of Leibniz's works. A brief word on these two aims is in order.

As I noted above, Leibniz wrote no single work that treated the whole of his philosophical system. Despite this it is often tempting to treat one or two of his writings as being generally representative of his thought as a whole, for the sake of convenience if nothing else. This is a temptation that I think ought to be resisted. To get a reasonably adequate understanding of Leibniz's thought requires a student to consult many different texts from various stages in his career. In fact, piecing together Leibniz's thought is not unlike putting together a huge jigsaw. Around 50,000 of Leibniz's writings (totalling some 200,000 pages) have survived to the present day, with most of these being private letters and relatively short essays and notes. With so many texts to choose from, only an unfeasibly large anthology could hope to be truly representative of his thought. In selecting texts for this volume I have tried to choose those that would enable a newcomer to Leibniz to attain a good idea of some of his thoughts on some of the wide range of topics on which he wrote. I have opted not to include two of his most famous works, the *Discourse on Metaphysics* and the so-called *Monadology*, partly because I feel neither can be properly understood by a newcomer to Leibniz without a sizeable commentary,[2] and partly because perfectly serviceable translations of both can be found for free on various Internet sites.

No fewer than forty of the selections in this volume are appearing in English for the first time. Around a dozen or so others were previously only available in English in old and now hard to find anthologies, or other works that are not widely accessible to many students or scholars; by including them here, I hope they will reach a wider audience than they might otherwise have done.

In translating the selections in this volume I have tried to find the right balance between accuracy and elegance, with the former always taking priority where both could not be attained simultaneously.

Notes

1 Or rather re-introduced, since the atomic hypothesis was first proposed by the ancient Greeks Leucippus, Democritus and Epicurus.

2 A view in some way vindicated by the fact that both are available in separate editions with sizeable commentaries.

I. METAPHYSICS

A. Creation[1]

1. On first truths (middle–end 1680)[2]

Absolutely first truths[3] are, among truths of reason, those which are identical, and among truths of fact this, from which all experiences can be demonstrated *a priori*, namely: everything possible demands existence, and hence will exist unless something else prevents it, which also demands existence and is incompatible with the former. It follows from this that that combination of things always exists by which the greatest possible number of things exists, so that if we assume *A, B, C, D* to be equal with regard to essence, i.e. equally perfect, or equally demanding existence, and if we assume that *D* is incompatible with *A* and with *B*, while *A* is compatible with any except *D*, and similarly with regard to *B* and *C*, it follows that this combination, *A, B, C*, excluding *D*,[4] will exist; for if we wish *D* to exist, it will not be able to coexist with anything except *C*, therefore the combination *C, D* will exist, which is certainly more imperfect than the combination *A, B, C*. And so it is obvious that things exist in the most perfect way. This proposition: *everything possible demands existence*,[5] can be proved *a posteriori*, by assuming that something exists; for either all things exist, and then every possible will demand existence to such an extent that it actually exists, or some things do not exist, and then a reason must be given why some things exist in place of others. But this cannot be given otherwise than from a general reason of essence or possibility, assuming that the possible demands existence by its own nature, and even in proportion to its possibility or according to its degree of essence. Unless in the nature of essence itself there is some inclination to exist, nothing would exist; for to say that some essences have this inclination and others do not, is to say something without a reason, since existence seems to be generally traced back to every essence in the same way.[6] But it is as yet unknown to men, whence arises the incompossibility of diverse things, or how it can happen that diverse essences are opposed to each other, seeing that all purely positive terms seem to be mutually compatible.

Truths which are first in respect of us are experiences.

Every truth which is not an absolutely first truth can be demonstrated from an absolutely first truth.

Every truth can be demonstrated either from absolutely first truths (and it is demonstrable that these are indemonstrable), or is itself an absolutely first truth. And this is what I usually say, nothing must be asserted without a reason, or rather nothing happens without a reason.

2. On the reason why these things exist rather than other things (March–August 1689)[7]

The same reason that brings it about that these things exist rather than other things, also brings it about that something exists rather than nothing. For if a reason is given why these things exist, the reason given will also be why anything exists. This reason is the prevalence of reasons for existence, compared with the reasons for non-existence, that is, to say it in a word, in the essences' demanding of existence, so that those things will exist which are not impeded. For indeed, if nothing demands existence, there would be no reason for existing. But assuming that all things demand existence, the existence of some things follows, for although all things may not be able to exist, the existence of those things follows through which most things co-exist. For example, if *a* and *b* and also *c* were equal, and *a* were incompatible with *b* and with *c*, but *b* were incompatible with *a* and compatible with *c*, and similarly *c* were incompatible with *a* and compatible with *b*, it would follow that all three *a*, *b*, *c* would not exist at the same time, and neither would one alone, *a* or *b* or *c*, but two, and of the various pairs *ab* would not exist, nor *ac*, but only *bc*. From this it is evident that every possible tends to existence in itself, but that it is impeded by accident, and that there are no other reasons for not existing, unless they arise from connected reasons for existing.

However, there must be in reality an existing source of existence-demanding essences; otherwise there will be nothing in essences except a figment of the mind, and since nothing follows from nothing, there will be a perpetual and necessary 'nothing'. But this source cannot be anything other than the necessary being, the foundation of essences, the origin of existences, i.e. God, acting most perfectly, because all things are in him and come from him; and indeed they do so voluntarily, but nevertheless in a manner determined towards what is best; therefore he chooses that which greater perfection demands in the coming together of those things which demand existence, and this coming together happens by the fact that the first cause has such wisdom and power that it gives occasion and strength to the highest reason; it is real and has effect. For essences do not make their way to existence except in God and through God, so that there is in God the reality of essences, or of eternal truths, and the production of existents, or of contingent truths.

3. On the ultimate origination of things (23 November 1697)[8]

Besides the world or aggregate of finite things, there is a certain dominant unity, not only as the soul is dominant in me, or rather as the self is dominant in my body, but also in a much more noble way. For the dominant unity of the universe not only rules the world, but also constructs or makes it; and it is superior to the world and, so to speak, extramundane, and it is thus the ultimate reason of things. For a sufficient reason for existence cannot be found in any single thing alone, nor in the whole aggregate and series of things. Let us imagine that the book of the elements of geometry has always existed, one always copied from another; it is evident that, even if a reason can be given for the present book from a past one, from which it was copied, nevertheless we shall never come upon a full reason no matter how many past books we assume, since we would always be right to wonder why such books have existed from all time, why books existed at all, and why they were written in this way. What is true of books is also true of the different states of the world; for a subsequent state is in a way copied from a preceding one (although according to certain laws of change). And so, however far back you go to earlier states, you will never find in those states a full reason why there should be any world rather than none, and why it should be such as it is.

Therefore, even if you should imagine the world eternal, because you still suppose only a succession of states, and because you will not find a sufficient reason in any of them, and indeed no matter how many states you assume you will not make the least progress towards giving a reason, it is evident that the reason must be sought elsewhere. For in eternal things, even if there is no cause, we must nevertheless realize that there is a reason, which in persisting things is their very necessity or essence, but in the series of changeable things, if this is imagined *a priori*[9] to be eternal, it would be the very prevailing of inclinations, as will soon be clear, whereby reasons do not necessitate (by an absolute or metaphysical necessity, where the contrary implies a contradiction), but incline. From this it is evident that not even by supposing the eternity of the world can we escape the ultimate, extramundane reason of things, i.e. God.

Therefore the reasons for the world lie hidden in something extramundane, different from the chain of states, or the series of things, the aggregate of which constitutes the world. And so we must pass from a physical or hypothetical necessity, which determines the later states of the world from the earlier, to something which is of absolute or metaphysical necessity, for which a reason cannot be given. For the present world is physically or hypothetically necessary, but not absolutely or metaphysically necessary. That is, by assuming that the world was ever in such and such a state, it follows that such and such states will arise in future. Therefore since the ultimate ground must be in something which is of metaphysical necessity, and there is no reason for an existing thing except from an existing thing, it follows that some single being must exist of metaphysical necessity, i.e. one whose essence is existence. And thus something exists that is different from the plurality of beings, i.e. from the world, which, as we have granted and shown, is not of metaphysical necessity.

But in order to explain a little more distinctly how temporal, contingent, or physical truths arise from eternal or essential or metaphysical truths, we must first acknowledge, from the fact that something exists rather than nothing, that there is in possible things, i.e. in possibility or essence itself, a certain demand for existence or (so to speak) a straining to exist, or (if I may so put it) a claim to exist; and, to sum up in a word, essence in itself strives for existence. From this it follows further that all possible things, i.e. things expressing an essence or possible reality, strive with equal right for existence[10] in proportion to their quantity of essence or reality, or to the degree of perfection which they contain; for perfection is nothing other than quantity of essence.

Hence it is very clearly understood that out of the infinite combinations of possibles, and possible series, there exists one through which the greatest amount of essence or possibility is brought into existence. There is always in things a principle of determination which must be sought in maximum and minimum; namely, that the greatest effect should be produced with the least expenditure, so to speak. And here the time, the place, or in a word the receptivity or capacity of the world, can be considered as the expenditure or the land on which a building is to be constructed as fittingly as possible, while the variety of forms correspond to the fitness of the building and to the number and elegance of its rooms. And the situation is like that in certain games where all the spaces on the board are to be filled according to certain rules, and where, unless you use some skill, you will in the end be excluded from certain spaces and forced to leave more spaces empty than you could have or wished to. But there is a definite rule through which the maximum number of spaces is most easily filled. For instance, if we were to suppose that a decision has been made to construct a triangle, without there being any other principle of determination, then it follows that an equilateral triangle is produced; and assuming that a move is to be made from one point to another, although nothing further determines the path between them, the easiest or shortest way will be chosen. Likewise, once it is assumed that being prevails over non-being, i.e. that there is a reason why something should exist rather than nothing, or that there is to be a transition from possibility to actuality, it follows that even if nothing further is determined, there exists as much as is possible in accordance with the capacity of time and space (or of the order of possible existence); in short it is just like tiles that are arranged so that as many as possible occupy a given area.

From these considerations it is now wonderfully evident how a certain divine mathematics or metaphysical mechanics is employed in the very origination of things, and how a determination of the maximum holds good, just as, of all the angles, the right angle is the determinate angle in geometry, and as liquids placed in other liquids organize themselves into the most capacious shape, namely the spherical; but especially as in common mechanics itself, when several heavy bodies are struggling against each another such a motion finally arises through which occurs the maximum descent on the whole. For just as all possibles strive with equal right for existence in proportion to their reality, so all heavy things strive with equal right to descend in proportion to their weight, and just as in the latter case a motion arises that consists of the greatest possible descent of heavy things, so in the former case a world arises through which the maximum production of possibles takes place.

And so we now have physical necessity from metaphysical necessity, for although the world is not metaphysically necessary, where its contrary would imply a contradiction or logical absurdity, nevertheless it is physically necessary, that is, determined so that its contrary would imply imperfection or moral absurdity. And just as possibility is the principle of essence, so perfection or degree of essence (through which the greatest number of things are compossible) is the principle of existence. From this it is also evident how there may be freedom in the author of the world, even though he does everything determinately: because he acts according to the principle of wisdom or perfection. Indifference, of course, arises from ignorance, and the wiser someone is, the more he is determined to do what is most perfect.

But (you will say) this comparison of a certain metaphysical determining mechanism with the physical mechanism of heavy bodies, elegant though it seems, is nevertheless weak insofar as striving heavy bodies really exist, but possibilities or essences before or beyond existence are imaginary or fictitious, and therefore no reason for existence can be sought in them. I answer that neither those essences, nor the so-called eternal truths about them, are fictitious, but that they exist in a certain region of ideas, so to speak, namely in God himself, the source of every essence and existence of other things. The very existence of the actual series of things indicates that we seem not to have spoken gratuitously. For since a reason is not found in the series, as we have shown above, but must be sought in metaphysical necessities or eternal truths, and existing things cannot exist except from existing things, as we have noted above, it must be the case that eternal truths have their existence in some absolutely or metaphysically necessary subject, that is, in God, through whom these truths, which otherwise would be imaginary, are realized, to use a barbarous but distinctive word.

But also we actually find that everything happens in the world according to the laws of the eternal truths, not only geometrical but also metaphysical laws, that is, not only according to material necessities, but also according to formal necessities; and not only is that true in general, with regard to that reason which we have now explained why the world exists rather than not, and why it exists thus rather than otherwise (which is to be sought in the striving of possibles for existence), but also when we come down to specific cases, we see the wonderful way in which metaphysical laws of cause, power, and action hold in the whole of nature, and that they prevail over the purely geometrical laws of matter, as I discovered to my great astonishment when giving an account of the laws of motion; indeed they prevail to such an extent that I was finally forced to abandon the law of the geometrical composition of endeavours, which I formerly defended in my youth (when I was more materialistic), as I have more adequately explained elsewhere.

So now we have the ultimate reason for the reality of both essences and existences in a unity, which is of necessity greater, superior, and prior to the world itself, since through it not only existing things, which make up the world, but also possible things have their reality. But because of the interconnection of all these things with each other, this ultimate reason can only be found in a single source. Moreover, it is evident that from this source existent things are continually flowing and are being produced and have been produced, since it is not clear why one state of the world more than another, yesterday's more than today's, should flow from this source. It is also evident how God acts not only physically but also freely, and that there must be in him not only the efficient but also the final cause, and so in him we have the reason not only for the greatness or power in the mechanism of the universe now established, but also for the goodness or wisdom in establishing it.

And lest anyone should think that moral perfection or goodness is confused here with metaphysical perfection or greatness, and should grant the latter while denying the former, it should be pointed out that it follows from what I have said not only that the world is the most perfect physically, or if you prefer, metaphysically, i.e. that that series of things has been produced which actually contains as much reality as possible, but also that the world must be the most perfect morally, because moral perfection is in fact physical perfection in minds themselves. Hence the world is not only the most admirable machine, but also insofar as it consists of minds it is the best commonwealth, through which there is conferred on minds as much happiness or joy as possible, and it is in this that their physical perfection consists.

But, you will say, in the world we find the opposite of this, since the worst very often happens to the best, innocent beasts as well as innocent men are broken and killed, even with torture, and finally the world, especially if we look at the government of the human race, seems to be a confused chaos rather than something ordained by some supreme wisdom. So it seems at first sight, I admit: but on deeper examination the opposite is established. It is evident *a priori* from those very considerations which I have brought forward that there is in fact the greatest possible perfection of all things, and thus also of minds.

And indeed it is unreasonable, as the jurisconsults say, to judge unless the whole law has been examined. We know a small part of the eternity that stretches out to infinity, for how short is the memory of the several thousand years which history hands down to us. And yet out of so few experiences we rashly make judgement about the immeasurable and the eternal, just as men born and bred in prison or, if you prefer, in the subterranean salt mines of Sarmatia, might think that there was no other light in the world than that scanty light of their torches, which is scarcely sufficient to guide their steps. Look at a very beautiful picture, then cover up all but a small part. What will be evident in it, no matter how closely you look at it, but some confused chaos of colours, without selection, without art; indeed, the more you look at it the more chaotic it will seem. And yet when the covering is removed, you will see the whole picture from an appropriate position, and then you will see that what seemed to be thoughtlessly smeared on the canvas was in fact accomplished with the greatest skill by the author of the work. What the eyes discern in a painting is also what the ears discern in music. Indeed, distinguished masters of composition often mix dissonances with consonances so that a listener may be aroused and pricked, as it were, and as if anxious about the outcome, be so much more joyful when all is then restored to order. It is much like our taking delight in small dangers, or in the experience of misfortunes, our delight coming from the very sense of our own power or happiness or the act of showing off. Or it is like when we delight in the spectacle of tightrope-walking or sword-dancing because of the very fears that they inspire, and we laughingly half-let go of children as if we were going to throw them away; it was for this reason that an ape carried off Christian, King of Denmark, when he was still an infant wrapped in swaddling clothes, to the edge of a roof, and then, when everyone was anxious, the ape – as if laughing – put him back into his cradle unharmed. On the same principle it is insipid to always eat sweet things; sharp, sour, and even bitter things should be mixed in to excite the taste. He who has not tasted the bitter does not deserve the sweet, nor will he appreciate it in fact. This is the very law of enjoyment, that pleasure does not come from a uniform course, for this produces disgust and makes us dull, not joyful.

But what we have said here, about a part which can be disturbed without on the whole harming the harmony, should not be taken to mean that no account is taken of the parts, or that it is sufficient, as it were, that the world be perfect as a whole although the human race is wretched, and that there is in the universe no concern for justice or no account taken of us, as some suppose, who judge incorrectly about the totality of things. For we must realize that, just as in the best constituted commonwealth care is taken that as much good as possible is bestowed on individuals, so also the universe would be insufficiently perfect unless it took individuals into account as far as is consistent with preserving the harmony of the universe. In this matter no better measure could be established than the law of justice itself, which dictates that everyone should take a part of the perfection of the universe and of his own happiness in proportion to the measure of his own virtue and the extent to which his will is disposed towards[11] the common good. This is secured by what we call God's charity and love, in which alone the force and power of the Christian religion consists, according to the judgement of wise theologians. Nor should it seem remarkable that there should be so much deference to minds in the universe, since they bear the closest resemblance to the image of the supreme author, and their relation to him is not merely as machines to their maker (as it is with other things) but also as citizens to their prince. And they endure as long as the universe itself, and in a way they express the whole and concentrate it in themselves, so that it can be said that minds are total parts.

But with regard to the afflictions of men, especially of good men, we must hold for certain that they result in the greater good of these men, and this is true not only theologically, but also physically, just as a seed cast into the earth suffers before it bears fruit. And in general it can be said that afflictions are evil for a time, but in effect are good, since they are short cuts to greater perfection. Likewise in physics, the liquids which ferment slowly also improve more slowly, but those in which there is a greater disturbance improve more quickly by throwing off impure parts with greater force. And this is what you might call stepping back in order to make a leap forward with greater force (one steps back for a better leap). Therefore these things must be considered to be not only pleasing and consoling, but also most true. And in general I think that there is nothing truer than happiness, and nothing happier and sweeter than truth.

Furthermore, it must be recognized that there is a perpetual and most free progress of the whole universe towards a consummation of the universal beauty and perfection of the works of God, so that it is always advancing towards greater cultivation. Just as now a large part of our earth has received cultivation, and will receive it more and more. And though it is true that a certain part sometimes grows wild again, or is destroyed again and oppressed, this must nevertheless be taken in the same way as we interpreted affliction a little while earlier, namely that this very destruction and oppression is useful for achieving something greater, so that in a way we profit from our very loss.

And as for the objection that could be made: that if this were so the world should have become a paradise before now, the response is at hand: although many substances have already attained great perfection, nevertheless on account of the divisibility of the continuum to infinity there always remain in the abyss of things parts that are still asleep, which are to be awakened and driven on to greater and better things, and in a word, to better cultivation. And hence progress never comes to an end.

4. Letter to Johann Christian Schulenburg (29 March 1698)[12]

Without doubt boundaries or limits are of the essence of creatures, but limits are something privative and consist in the denial of further progress. At the same time it must be acknowledged that a creature, after a value is received from God and such as it affects the senses, also contains something positive or something beyond boundaries, and cannot in fact be resolved into mere limits or indivisibles. And hence I also think that what is postulated by the sense of the author's theses,[13] from which he infers the resolution into mere limits or mere indivisibles, cannot be applied to a creature taken with its value. And this value, since it must consist of a positive, is a certain degree of created perfection, to which the power of action also belongs, which in my view constitutes the nature of substance. So much so that this value bestowed by God is in fact the energy or power imparted to things, which some people deny in vain, not noticing that they themselves, contrary to their expectation, fall into the doctrine of Spinoza, who makes God the only substance and everything else modes of it.

0	0
1	1
10	2
11	3
100	4
101	5
110	6
111	7
1000	8

And this is the origin of things from God and nothing, positive and privative, perfection and imperfection, value and limits, active and passive, form (i.e. entelechy, endeavour, energy) and matter or mass which is in itself inactive, except insofar as it has resistance. I have made those things clear to some extent by the origin of numbers from 0 and 1, which I have observed is the most beautiful symbol of the continuous creation of things from nothing, and of their dependence on God. For when the simplest progression is used, namely the dyadic[14] instead of the decadic[15] or quaternary,[16] all numbers can be expressed by 0 and 1, as will be evident in the table I have added, and in this genesis of numbers, which is especially suitable for nature, many things lie hidden that are wonderful for contemplation, and indeed for practice, even though it is not for common use.

5. Letter to André Morell (4/14 May 1698)[17]

As all minds are unities, it can be said that God is the primitive unity, expressed by all the others according to their capacity. His goodness moved him to act, and there are in him three primacies: power, knowledge and will; the result of these is the operation or creature, which is varied according to the different combinations of unity and zero; or rather of the positive with the privative, for the privative is nothing other than limits, and there are limits everywhere in a creature, just as there are points everywhere in the line. However, a creature is something more than limits, because it has received some perfection or power from God, just as the line is something more than points. For ultimately the point (the end of the line) is nothing more than the negation of the progress beyond which it ends. I do not believe that there is a determined number of creatures, and in my opinion the court of the supreme Monarch is larger than one thinks . . . I think, moreover, that everything is animate, that all minds except God are embodied, and that the universe always develops for the better, or if it worsens it is only in order to make a better leap. Also, that every organized substance has in itself an infinity of others, and that it even has fellow creatures in its centre; that no substance will perish, and that those that are in the darkness of the centres will in their turn appear in the larger theatre.

B. Truth and Substance[18]

1. On the perfect concept of substances (1677?)[19]

A substance is a Being that involves all necessary predicates of the same subject, such as *air*. An adjunct is what does not involve everything, such as *transparent*. For *air* involves *transparent, clear, subtle, elastic,* etc., and nothing else concerning that thing of which 'air' is necessarily predicated, which is not already contained in the concept of air. There can be posited or can certainly be understood pure air, that is Being, about which nothing can be predicated other than what the nature of air requires; but pure transparency cannot be posited, that is Being in which there may be transparency and nothing else. Hence it seems to follow that substances alone should be called the lowest, or individual species – namely, those whose concept is perfect, or such that in that concept there is contained an answer to everything that can be asked about the thing. However the concept of an animal is not such a thing, for it can still be asked: is it rational or irrational, quadruped or biped, because some animals are rational and others are irrational. Unless perhaps we are to believe that a pure animal can be posited, or one in which nothing is found other than what is precisely required for the concept of an animal, and therefore we may wish to call an animal a substance because at any rate its concept is able to subsist by itself. But I very much doubt that a pure animal is possible. For not only will it be without feet, but also sensation, because the concept of an animal does not express what it should sense. Therefore only those general terms which are homogeneous are of substances, and such is the concept of pure or absolute Being, i.e. the concept of God.

2. The principle of human knowledge (winter 1685/1686?)[20]

Just as when building a house in a sandy place we must continue digging until we hit upon solid rock or firm foundations; and when unravelling a tangled thread we must look for the beginning; and when the greatest weights had to be moved Archimedes demanded only a stable place; likewise to establish the elements of human knowledge some fixed point is needed on which we can safely lean and from which we can safely proceed.

I think that this principle is to be sought in the general nature of truths, and that we should hold this above all: *every proposition is either true or false*. A proposition is false which is contradictory of the true. *Contradictory propositions*, however, are those which do not differ in any other way than that one of them is affirmative, the other negative. And these principles are such that it is pointless to demand a proof of them. For since we can only bring forward other propositions as proofs, they will obviously be brought forward in vain if they can be granted and denied at the same time, or be simultaneously true and false, and every inquiry into truth would cease immediately from the start. Further, every time that some proposition is used it is thought to be true, unless otherwise advised.

A true proposition is one whose predicate is contained in its subject, or more generally one whose consequent is contained in its antecedent, and hence it is necessary that there be some connection between the concepts of the terms, i.e. that there be an objective foundation from which the reason of the proposition can be given or an *a priori* proof can be found. And it holds in the case of every true affirmative proposition, universal or singular, necessary or contingent, that the concept of the predicate is in the concept of the subject, either expressly or virtually; expressly in the case of an identical proposition, virtually in the case of any other. And the predicate of the proposition can be proved from the subject, or the consequent from the antecedent, by the resolution either of the antecedent or subject alone, or of both the antecedent and consequent simultaneously, or of the subject and predicate simultaneously. And indeed, the connection is necessary in the case of propositions of eternal truth, which follow from ideas alone or from definitions of universal ideas. But if a proposition is contingent there is no necessary connection, but it varies in time and depends on an assumed divine decree and on free will. And in that case a reason can always be given (at least by one who knows all) from the nature of the thing, or from the concept of the terms, why what has been done has been done, rather than not done. But that reason only inclines, and does not impose necessity. From this there follows an axiom of the greatest use, from which many things in physics and in morals are derived: *nothing happens for which a reason cannot be given why it should happen thus rather than otherwise.*

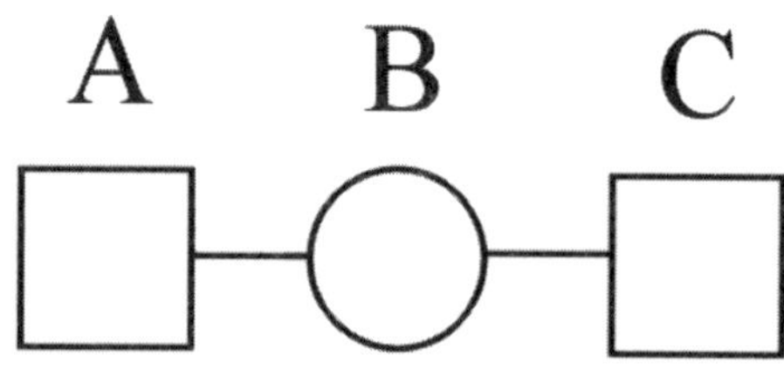

For example, it is assumed by Archimedes that among the foundations of the whole of statics, two equal weights A and B, equally distant from the centre of motion C, are in equilibrium, which is a corollary of our axiom; for if any difference comes to pass, then certainly some reason for the difference can be given (by our axiom) which cannot happen (according to the hypothesis), since everything on both sides is assumed to be in the same state, and so nothing diverse can follow from this.

Therefore, when we have understood that every proposition is either true or false, and that every true proposition which is not true through itself, or immediate, can be proved *a priori*, it follows that we should explain the method of proof. This is in fact chiefly contained in the axiom: *without impairing the truth, the predicate can be substituted in place of the subject of a universal affirmative proposition, or the consequent in place of the antecedent of an affirmative proposition, in another proposition where the subject of the former proposition is the predicate, or where the antecedent of the former is the consequent.* But we must make an exception of reduplicative propositions, in which we show that we speak so strictly about some term that we do not want another to be substituted in its place. For these propositions are reflexive, and in respect of our thoughts are as material propositions in respect of speech. Besides, the reason for this axiom is evident from the preceding analysis. For let us suppose that there is a universal affirmative proposition, *every B is C*, and another proposition, *A is B*. I say that in the latter, *C* can be substituted for *B*, for since *A* contains *B* and *B* contains *C* (by the preceding axiom), *A* will also contain *C*, which is sufficient (by the same axiom) for us to say that *A* is *C*. But I do not wish to pursue here the variety of propositions and to propound logical rules, for it is sufficient to have indicated the foundation of substitution.

If some concept is complete, i.e. is such that from it a reason can be given for all the predicates of the same subject to which this concept can be attributed, it will be the concept of an individual substance, and vice versa. For an individual substance is a subject which is not in another subject, but others are in it, and so all the predicates of the same subject are all the predicates of the same individual substance. For these predicates, therefore, a reason can be given from the concept of the individual substance, and from that alone, as is clear from the second axiom. And so the concept which is responsible for this is the concept of the individual substance itself.

3. Remarks on Mr Arnauld's letter concerning my proposition: that the individual concept of each person contains once and for all everything that will ever happen to him (May 1686)[21]

He admits in good faith that he took my opinion to be that all an individual's events are deducible from its individual concept in the same way and with the same necessity that the properties of a sphere are deducible from its specific concept or definition; and that I had considered the concept of the individual in itself, without regard for the manner in which it exists in God's understanding or will. *For* (he says) *it appears to me that we are not accustomed to consider the specific concept of a sphere in relation to how it is represented in the divine understanding, but in relation to what it is in itself, and I supposed it was the same with the individual concept of each person; but he adds that, now that he knows what my thinking is on this, that is enough to allow him to try to find out whether it removes all the difficulties;*[22] something which he still doubts. I see that Mr Arnauld has not remembered, or at least not concerned himself with the opinion of the Cartesians, who hold that God establishes by his will the eternal truths, such as are those that concern the properties of the sphere; but as I am not of their opinion any more than Mr Arnauld is, I will merely say why I believe that we must philosophize differently about the concept of an individual substance than we do about the specific concept of a sphere. The reason is that while the concept of a *species* only contains eternal or necessary truths, the concept of an individual contains *sub ratione possibilitatis* [under the aspect of possibility] what is fact, or what is related to the existence of things and to time, and consequently it depends on some of God's free decrees, considered as possible. For truths of fact or of existence depend upon God's decrees. Thus the concept of a sphere in general is incomplete or abstract, which is to say that only the essence of a sphere in general or in theory is considered, without regard to individual circumstances, and consequently the concept does not in any way contain what is required for the existence of a certain sphere. But the concept of the sphere that Archimedes had placed upon his tomb is a complete concept, and must contain everything that belongs to the subject of that form. This is why in individual considerations, or in practical matters, *quae versantur circa singularia* [which turn on individual things], besides the form of the sphere the matter of which it is made enters into it, as does the place, the time, and the other circumstances, which by a continual chain would ultimately include the whole sequence of the universe, if it were possible to trace out everything that these concepts contain. For the concept of this piece of matter from which this sphere is made includes all the changes that it has undergone or will undergo in future. And in my opinion, each individual substance always contains the traces of whatever has happened to it, and the marks of whatever will ever happen to it. But what I have just said may be sufficient to explain the thought process behind this . . .

It appears obvious to us that this square of marble brought from Genoa would have been exactly the same even if it had been left there, because our senses only make us judge superficially; but ultimately, because of the connection of things, the whole universe with all its parts would be very different, and would have been a different one from the beginning if the least thing in it went differently from how it does go. On account of this, it is not the case that events are necessary, but it is the case that they are certain, given the choice that God made of this possible universe, whose concept contains this sequence of things. I hope that what I am going to say will make even Mr Arnauld agree with this.

Let a straight line A B C represent a certain time, and let a certain individual substance, myself for example, endure or subsist during this time. Firstly, then, let us consider the me who subsists during the time A B, and also the me who subsists during the time B C. Because we suppose that it is the same individual substance which endures, or rather that it is me who subsists during the time A B while I am in Paris, and that it is also me who subsists during the time B C while I am in Germany, there must necessarily be some reason why we can truly say that we persist, that is to say that I, who was in Paris, am now in Germany. For if there were no reason for it, we would have as much right to say it was someone else. It is true that my internal experience convinced me *a posteriori* of this identity, but there must also be an *a priori* reason for it. Now it is not possible to find another reason if it is not the case that my attributes of the preceding time and state as well as my attributes of the succeeding time and state are predicates of one and the same subject, *insunt eidem subjecto* [they belong to the same subject]. Now what is it to say that the predicate is in the subject if not that the concept of the predicate is in some manner included in the concept of the subject? And because from the moment I began to exist it could be truly said of me that this or that would happen to me, we must accept that these predicates were laws contained in the subject or in my complete concept, which makes what is called 'me' and is the basis of the connection of all my different states, which God knew perfectly from all eternity. After that I think that all doubts must vanish, for in saying that the individual concept of Adam entails everything that will ever happen to him, I mean to say no more than what all philosophers understand when they say *praedicatum inesse subjecto verae propositionis* [the predicate belongs to the subject of true propositions] . . .

I agree that in order to judge of the concept of an individual substance it is good to consider the concept that I have of myself, just as we should consider the specific concept of the sphere in order to judge of its properties, although there is a great difference here. For the concept of myself and of every other individual substance is infinitely more extensive and difficult to comprehend than a specific concept, as is the concept of the sphere, which is merely incomplete. It is not enough that I sense myself to be a substance which thinks, one would have to conceive distinctly what distinguishes me from all other minds; but I have only a confused experience of it. Consequently, although it is easy to judge that the number of feet in the diameter is not contained in the concept of the sphere in general, it is not so easy to judge whether the journey I intend to make is contained in my concept, otherwise it would be as easy for us to be prophets as geometers. I am uncertain as to whether I will make the journey, but I am certain that whether I do so or not I will always be myself. This is a prejudice which must not be confused with a distinct concept or item of knowledge. These things appear undetermined to us only because their advance signs or marks in our substance are not recognizable to us. It is more or less as those who only consider their senses will call a fool the one who tells them that the smallest movement is communicated as far as matter extends, because experience alone cannot demonstrate it; yet when one considers the nature of motion and matter one is convinced of it. It is the same here: when one considers only the confused experience that one has of one's individual concept in particular, one is far from perceiving this connection of events; but when one considers the general and distinct concepts that are involved, one finds that connection. Indeed, when I consider the concept that I have of every true proposition, I find that every necessary or contingent predicate, past, present, or future, is included in the concept of the subject, and I ask no more of it.

I even believe that this will open up a path of conciliation for us, for I imagine that Mr Arnauld was reluctant to grant this proposition only because he took the connection that I support to be a connection that was intrinsic and necessary at the same time, while I hold that it is intrinsic but by no means necessary; for I have now sufficiently explained that it is based on free decrees and acts. I understand no other connection between subject and predicate than the one found in the most contingent truths, that is to say that there is always something to conceive in the subject which serves to explain why this predicate or event pertains to it, or why this has happened rather than not. But these reasons for contingent truths incline without necessitating. It is therefore true that I would be able not to make this journey, but it is certain that I will do so. This predicate or event is not with certainty linked with my other predicates conceived incompletely or taken generally; but it is certainly linked with my complete individual concept, since I suppose that this concept is expressly fashioned so that everything that happens to me can be deduced from it, and it doubtless exists objectively, and is properly the concept of myself in different states, since it is this concept alone which can include them all . . .

The proposition in question is of very great importance and deserves to be well established, for it follows that every soul is like a world apart, independent of everything except for God; that it is not only immortal and so to speak impassable, but retains in its substance traces of everything that happens to it. It also shows us in what consists the commerce of substances, and especially the union of the soul and the body. This commerce does not come about in accordance with the ordinary hypothesis of a physical influence of one on the other, for each present state of a substance occurs in it spontaneously and is merely a consequence of its preceding state. Nor does the commerce come about in accordance with the hypothesis of occasional causes, which holds that God routinely interferes in things beyond his conservation of each substance in its course, and that God produces thoughts in the soul on the occasion of something taking place in the body, which would change the course that it would have taken without his interference. But the commerce does happen in accordance with the hypothesis of concomitance, which appears to me to be demonstrative. That is to say, every substance expresses the whole sequence of the universe in accordance with its own viewpoint or the relation proper to it, from which it happens that they agree perfectly.

4. Letter to Antoine Arnauld (4/14 July 1686)[23]

The fact is that in every true affirmative proposition, necessary or contingent, universal or particular, the concept of the predicate is always in some way included in that of the subject, *praedicatum inest subjecto* [the predicate is included in the subject], or else I do not know what truth is.

Now, I do not ask for more of a connection here than that which objectively exists between the terms of a true proposition, and it is only in this sense that I say that the concept of the individual substance contains all its events and all its denominations, even those that are commonly called extrinsic (that is to say, those that only belong to it by virtue of the general connection of things, and from the fact that it expresses the entire universe in its own way), because *there must always be some basis for the connection of the terms of a proposition, which must be found in their concepts.* This is my great principle, with which I believe all philosophers must agree, and of which one of the corollaries is the common axiom that nothing happens without a reason, and that one can always explain why a thing turned out thus rather than otherwise, although this reason often inclines without necessitating, a perfect indifference being a chimerical or incomplete supposition. It is evident that I draw surprising consequences from the aforesaid principle, but it is only because people are not accustomed to pursue the clearest knowledge far enough.

Besides, the proposition which has given rise to all this discussion is very important and deserves to be well established, for it follows that every individual substance expresses the entire universe in its way and from a certain angle, or according to the point of view from which it looks at the universe, so to speak; and that its succeeding state is a result (although free, or rather contingent) of its preceding state, as if there were only God and itself in the world. Thus each individual substance or complete being is like a world apart, independent of every other thing besides God. There is no stronger argument for demonstrating not only the indestructibility of our soul, but also that it always retains in its nature the traces of all its preceding states with a potential memory which can always be roused, because the soul has consciousness, or knows in itself what everyone calls 'I'. This renders it susceptible of moral qualities, and of punishment and reward, even after this life. For immortality without memory would be of no use to it. But this independence does not prevent the commerce of substances with one another; for as all created substances are a continual production of the same sovereign being in accordance with the same plans, and as they express the same universe or the same phenomena, they perfectly agree with each other, and that makes us say that one acts upon the other, because one expresses more distinctly than the other the cause or reason for the changes, in much the same way that we attribute motion to the ship rather than to the whole sea, and rightly so, although speaking abstractly we could maintain another hypothesis of motion, since motion in itself, leaving aside the cause, is always something relative. In my opinion this is how we must understand the commerce of created substances with one another, and not as a real physical influence or dependence, which we could never conceive distinctly.

5. Logical-metaphysical principles (spring–summer 1689?)[24]

Primary truths are those which express the same thing of itself, or deny the opposite of its opposite, such as *A is A*, or *A is not not-A*. If it is true that *A is B*, it is false that *A is not B*, or that *A is not-B*. Likewise, *each thing is what it is, each thing is like itself or is equal to itself, nothing is greater or less than itself*, and others of this kind which, although they may have their own degrees of priority, nevertheless can all be covered by the one name of 'identities'.

Moreover, all remaining truths are reduced to primary truths by the help of definitions, i.e. through the resolution of concepts, in which consists *a priori proof*, independent of experience. I shall give as an example a proposition accepted as axiomatic by mathematicians and all others alike: *the whole is greater than its part, or a part is less than the whole*, which is very easily demonstrated from the definition of 'less' or 'greater', with the addition of the primitive axiom, the one of identity. For the 'less' is that which is equal to a part of another ('greater') thing, which is certainly a definition very easy to understand and is consistent with the practice of the human race, when men compare things to each other, and find the excess by taking away something equal to the lesser from the greater. Hence we get this sort of argument: a part is equal to a part of the whole (namely to itself, since by the axiom of identity each thing is equal to itself). But what is equal to a part of the whole is less than the whole (by the definition of 'less'). Therefore a part is less than the whole.

Therefore the predicate or consequent is always in the subject or antecedent, and the nature of truth in general, i.e. the connection between the terms of a proposition, consists in this very thing, as Aristotle has also observed. And indeed, in identities this connection and inclusion of the predicate in the subject is explicit, whereas in all other truths it is implicit and must be shown through the analysis of concepts, on which *a priori* demonstration is founded.

Moreover, this is true of every affirmative truth, universal or particular, necessary or contingent, and in the case of both an intrinsic and extrinsic denomination. And here lies hidden a wonderful secret in which is contained the nature of contingency, or the essential difference between necessary and contingent truths, and through which the difficulty about the fatal necessity of things, even those which are free, is removed.

From these things, which are insufficiently considered because of their very great obviousness, there follow many things of great importance, for from this there at once arises the accepted axiom, *nothing exists without a reason*, or *there is no effect without a cause*. Otherwise there would be a truth which could not be proved *a priori*, i.e. which could not be resolved into identities, which is contrary to the nature of truth, which is always either explicitly or implicitly identical. It also follows from this that when everything in one part of the data is the same as in another part, then everything will also be the same on both sides in what is sought, i.e. in the consequences, because no reason can be given for a difference, which must be sought from the data. And a corollary, or rather an example of this, is Archimedes' postulate at the beginning of his book on equilibrium,[25] that when the arms of a balance and the weights placed on each side are equal, everything is in a state of equilibrium. Hence *there is a reason even for eternal things*. If we imagine that the world has existed from eternity, and that there have been only globes in it, a reason must be given why there should be globes rather than cubes.

From this it also follows that *there cannot be in nature two individual things different in number alone*. For it certainly must be possible to give a reason why they are different, which must be found in some difference in them. And so what St. Thomas recognized about separate intelligences, which he said never differ in number alone,[26] must be said about other things too; and two eggs, or two leaves or blades of grass, perfectly similar to each other, will never be found. Therefore perfect similarity occurs only in incomplete and abstract concepts, where things are not considered in all respects, but only according to a certain mode of consideration, such as when we just consider shapes, and neglect the shaped matter. Consequently geometers rightly consider two triangles to be similar, even though two perfectly similar material triangles are never found. And although gold and other metals, salts, and many liquids are considered as homogeneous bodies, that can be admitted only so far as our senses are concerned, and as such it is not exactly true that they are homogeneous.

It also follows that *there are no purely extrinsic denominations,* which have absolutely no foundation in the thing denominated. For it is necessary that the concept of the subject denominated contain the concept of the predicate. And hence whenever the denomination of a thing is changed, there must be some variation that occurs in the thing itself.

The complete or perfect concept of an individual substance contains all of its predicates, past, present and future. For certainly it is true now that a future predicate is future, and so is contained in the concept of the thing. And hence all the things that will happen to Peter or Judas, both necessary and free, are contained in the perfect individual concept of Peter or Judas, considered within the realm of possibility by abstracting the mind from the divine decree to create him, and these things are seen by God. And hence it is evident that God chooses, from an infinity of possible individuals, those which he thinks are most consistent with the supreme and hidden ends of his wisdom, and, if we are speaking accurately, he does not decree that Peter sin, or that Judas be damned, but only that a Peter who would sin (certainly indeed, though not necessarily but freely) and a Judas who would suffer damnation, should come into existence in preference to other possibles, i.e. that a possible concept should become actual. And although the future salvation of Peter is also contained in his eternal possible concept, it is, however, not without the concourse of grace, for in the same perfect concept of this possible Peter, even the assistance of the divine grace that is to be given to him is contained within his possible concept.

Every individual substance contains in its perfect concept the whole universe, and everything existing in it, past, present and future. For there is no thing on which some true denomination cannot be imposed from another, at any rate a denomination of comparison and relation. But there is no purely extrinsic denomination. I show the same thing in many other ways that are in harmony with each other.

Indeed, *all created individual substances are different expressions of the same universe,* and of the very same universal cause, namely God. But the expressions vary in perfection, like different representations or drawings of the same town from different points of view.

Every created individual substance exercises physical action and passion on all the others. For when a change occurs in one, there follows some corresponding change in all the others, because the denomination is changed. And this is consistent with our experience of nature, for we see that in a vessel full of liquid (and the whole universe is such a vessel) a motion brought about in the middle is propagated to the edges, although it is rendered more and more insensible as it recedes further from its origin.

It can be said, strictly speaking, that *no created substance exercises a metaphysical action or influx on another*. For, leaving aside the fact that it is impossible to explain how anything passes over from one thing into the substance of another, it has already been shown that from the concept of any particular thing all its future states already follow. And what we call 'causes' are only concomitant requisites, in metaphysical rigour. This very thing is made clear by our experiences of nature, for bodies actually move back from other bodies by the force of their own elasticity and not by any outside force, even if another body is required in order that the elasticity (which arises from something intrinsic to the body itself) be able to act.

Also, with the distinction of soul and body assumed, their union can be explained from this without the common hypothesis of an influx, which is unintelligible, and without the hypothesis of an occasional cause, which invokes a *Deus ex machina*. For God has from the beginning established soul and body alike with such wisdom and such skill that, from the very first constitution or concept of each thing, everything that happens in itself in one corresponds perfectly to everything that happens in the other, just as if they had passed over from one into the other. I call this the *hypothesis of concomitance*, which holds true of all substances in the whole universe, but it is not perceptible in all of them, as it is in the soul and the body.

There is no vacuum. For the different parts of an empty space would be perfectly similar and mutually congruent, and could not be distinguished from each other, and thus would differ in number alone, which is absurd. In the same way in which it is proved that space is not a thing, it is proved that time is not a thing either.[27]

There is no atom, indeed there is no body so small that it is not actually subdivided. On account of that, while it is acted upon by all the other things in the whole universe, and receives some effect from everything else, which must bring about a change in the body, it has also preserved all past impressions and contains in advance its future impressions. And if anyone says that the effect is contained in the motions impressed on the atom, which receives the effect in the whole without its division, we can reply to this that not only must effects result in the atom from all the impressions of the universe, but also the state of the whole universe must in turn be inferred from the atom, and from the effect the cause. But from the shape and motion of an atom alone we cannot infer by regression the impressions by which the motion has reached it, because the same motion can be obtained from different impressions. Not to mention the fact that no reason can be given why bodies of a certain smallness should not be further divisible.

From this it follows that *a world of infinite creatures is contained in every particle of the universe.* Nevertheless the continuum is not divided into points, nor is it divided in all possible ways. Not into points, because points are not parts, but limits; not in all possible ways, because not all creatures are in the same part, but only a certain progression of them to infinity, just as he who assumes a straight line and any bisected part of it establishes different divisions from he who assumes a trisected part.

There is no actual determinate shape in things, for no shape can satisfy infinite impressions. And so neither a circle, nor an ellipse, nor any other line definable by us exists except in the intellect, nor do lines before they are drawn, or parts before they are cut off.

Extension and motion, and even bodies themselves, insofar as the former occur in the latter alone, are not substances but true phenomena, like rainbows and parhelia. For shapes do not exist objectively, and bodies, if we consider their extension alone, are not one substance but many.

For the substance of bodies something without extension is required; otherwise there will be no principle of the reality of phenomena, or of true unity. Bodies are always held to be a plurality, never one, and therefore there is not actually a plurality. Cordemoy proved atoms with a similar argument, but as atoms are excluded there remains something lacking extension, analogous to the soul, which was once called form or species.

A corporeal substance can neither arise nor perish except by creation or annihilation, for if it once endures it will always endure, since there is no reason for any difference, and the dissolution of the parts of a body has nothing in common with its destruction. Therefore, *animated things do not arise or perish, but are only transformed.*

6. On body and substance truly one (March 1690)[28]

A body is not a substance, but an aggregate of substances. For it consists of many things that are really distinct, such as a pile of wood, a heap of stones, a flock, an army, a pool in which many fish swim; and each body is actually divided into the many distinct bodies that it contains.

Substances do not exist when a substance does not exist, and numbers do not exist unless there are unities, and so it is necessary that besides bodies there exist certain substances truly one, or indivisible, by whose aggregations bodies are formed.

The error of materialist philosophers lies in this, that when they acknowledged the necessity of unity they sought substance in matter, as if any body could exist that would in fact be one substance. And so they resort to atoms as the end of analysis. But since every body consists of diverse substances, it does not matter whether the parts are connected or not. Besides the fact that a reason for indivisibility cannot be found in atoms.

Therefore, since every body is a mass or aggregate of many bodies, no body is a substance; and hence we must look for substance outside of corporeal nature.

A substance, however, is something truly one, indivisible, and thus ingenerable and incorruptible, which is the subject of action and passion; and in short, what I understand when I say *I*, which subsists even though my body undergoes changes through its parts, as my body is certainly in a perpetual flux, while 'I' survive. No part of my body can be identified which is necessary for my subsistence, yet I am never without some united part of matter.

Nevertheless I have need of an organic body, although there is nothing in it that is necessary for my subsistence.

I recognize something analogous in every animal, and to say it in a word, in every true substance that is truly one.

But there are infinite simple substances or creatures in any particle of matter, and matter is composed from them, not as from parts, but as from constitutive principles, or from absolute requisites, exactly like points make up the essence of the continuum, though not as parts; for a part does not exist unless it is of the same sort as the whole, but substance is not of the same sort as matter or body any more than a point is of the same sort as a line.

In every substance there is nothing other than that nature or primitive force from which follows the series of its internal operations.

This series, i.e. all of its past and future states, can be recognized from any state of the substance, i.e. from its nature.

In addition, any given substance contains the whole universe, and the states of other things can be recognized from its states.

The series of diverse substances perfectly agree with each other, and each expresses the whole universe according to its own manner. And in this agreement consists the union of the soul and the body, and likewise that which we call the operation of substances outside each other.

The more perfect a substance is, the more distinctly it expresses the universe.

7. Letter to Pierre Dangicourt (1716)[29]

I am delighted that a mind as mathematical as yours applies itself also to philosophical research. This will help my aim of making philosophy demonstrative. It seems to me that our sentiments are not greatly far from each other. I am also of the opinion that, to speak precisely, there is no such thing as extended substance. That is why I call matter *non substantiam sed substantiatum* [not substance but substantiated].[30] I have said in some places (maybe in the *Theodicy*, if I am not mistaken) that matter is only a well-ordered and exact phenomenon, which is not deceptive if one pays attention to the abstract rules of reason. True substances are only simple substances, or what I call monads. And I believe that there are only monads in nature, everything else being only phenomena that result from them. Every monad is a mirror of the universe according to its point of view, and is accompanied by a multitude of other monads, which compose its organic body, of which it is the dominant monad. And in a monad there are only perceptions and tendencies to new perceptions and appetites, just as in the universe of phenomena there are only shapes and motion. The monad therefore already envelops its past and future states in itself, so that an omniscient being could read them from it; and monads agree between themselves, being mirrors of the same universe to infinity, although the universe itself is of an infinite diffusion. It is in this that consists my pre-established harmony. Monads (of which those known to us are called souls) change their state by themselves, in accordance with the laws of final causes or of appetites, and nevertheless the kingdom of final causes accords with the kingdom of efficient causes, which is that of phenomena. However I do not say that the continuum is composed of geometric points, for matter is not a continuum and continuous extension is only an ideal thing, consisting of possibilities, which does not have in it any actual parts. Purely intellectual entities have parts only potentially. Thus the straight line has actual parts only insofar as it is actually sub-divided to infinity, but if there were another order of things, the phenomena would cause it to be sub-divided in another way. It is like the unity in arithmetic which is also a purely intellectual or ideal entity divisible into parts, as for example into fractions, which are not actually in unity itself (otherwise it would be reducible to minimal parts that are not present in numbers at all), but depend on how we have designated fractions. I therefore say that matter, which is something actual, only results from monads, which is to say from simple indivisible substances, but that extension or geometric magnitude is not composed of the possible parts that can merely be assigned to it, nor is it resolvable into points, and that points are only extremities, and by no means parts or components of the line.

Notes

1 See also III.B.4, VI.B.1.

2 A VI iv 1442–3. Latin.

3 Leibniz wrote in the margin here: 'The definition of truth is real. Truth is what is demonstrable by definitions from identity. What is demonstrated from nominal definitions is hypothetically true, what is demonstrated from real definitions is absolutely true; only real definitions of these concepts that are immediately perceived by us can be adduced, as when I say *to exist, to be true, extension* and *heat*; for what we perceive confusedly is to be assigned to the latter and regarded as something distinct. Real definitions can be proved *a posteriori,* namely by experiences.'

4 Leibniz wrote in the margin here: 'That every existent is possible must be demonstrated from the definition of existence.'

5 Leibniz wrote in the margin here: 'If existence were something other than what is demanded by essence, it would follow that it would have a certain essence, or would add something new to things, about which it might be asked again, whether this essence exists or does not exist, and why that one rather than another.'

6 Leibniz wrote in the margin here: 'Because a true proposition is one which is identical, or it can be demonstrated from identities by using definitions, it follows that a real definition of existence consists in this, that what is the most perfect, or what involves more essence, does exist out of those things which are otherwise able to exist. So that it is the nature of possibility or essence to demand existence. Unless that were so, a reason for the existence of things could not be given.'

7 A VI iv 1634–5. Latin.

8 G VII 302–8. Latin.

9 Reading *a priori* for *a priore* (Gerhardt and Erdman).
10 Reading *existentiam* (Erdman) for *essentiam* (Gerhardt).
11 Reading *erga* (Erdman) for *ergo* (Gerhardt).
12 GM VII 239. Latin.
13 Leibniz is here referring to the work of a minor figure, Knoll.
14 I.e. the base 2 (binary) number system.
15 I.e. the base 10 (decimal) number system.
16 I.e. the base 4 number system.
17 A I xv 560–1. French.
18 See also II.B.2 and III.B.4.
19 A VI iv 1350–1. Latin.
20 A VI iv 670–2. Latin.
21 G II 39, 42–3, 45–7. French.
22 This is Leibniz's summary of Arnauld's own words, from Arnauld's letter to Leibniz of 13 May 1686 (G II 28).
23 G II 56–7. French.
24 A VI iv 1643–8. Latin.
25 Archimedes, *On the Equilibrium of Planes*, book 1, postulate 1.
26 Aquinas, *Summa Theologicae*, 1q50a4.
27 Leibniz originally wrote here: '*There is no corporeal substance to which nothing belongs but extension or size, shape and their variations*. For if this were so, two corporeal substances perfectly similar to each other could exist, which is absurd. From this it follows that there is something in corporeal substances analogous to the soul, which is called a form.'
28 A VI iv 1672–3. Latin.
29 E 745–6. French.
30 'I call "substantiated" an aggregate of substances, like an army of men or a flock of sheep, and all bodies are such aggregates', C 13.

II. MIND, BODY AND SOUL

A. Souls and Their Nature[1]

1. Difficulties concerning the nature and origin of souls (summer 1683–winter 1684/1685)[2]

There are many difficulties concerning the nature and origin of souls, whatever opinions we may eventually choose. If we say that rational creatures alone have souls or substantial forms, but not beasts or other bodies, then besides the fact that this is scarcely credible, it follows from this that bodies are not substances, but only phenomena, which seems to conflict with church dogmas. But if we also assign souls to beasts, we must ask about their nature and origin. And indeed, every substantial form or soul is indivisible by necessity, and cannot arise except by creation, or perish except by annihilation, and so it must be said either that the souls of beasts began with the world, or are continually created by God. If they were created immediately from the beginning and began with the world, it must also be said that the soul of the animal called man existed from the beginning, and all rational souls pre-existed in Adam or indeed with Adam, for it will not in fact be lower than the souls of beasts. From this it follows that there are many human souls which never reach the point where they become part of human bodies, which seems ridiculous; and it does not seem very agreeable to reason to say that those people who always retain their chastity did not have inside them the true seeds of human nature. But if it is said that the animal soul did indeed already exist from the beginning, and that it underwent many transformations, as animals are accustomed to do, but in the end a mind was added to it, it seems to follow that there are two substantial forms or souls in man, one animal, the other rational, which is likewise difficult to prove. For it is absurd to say that a human soul was made from a bestial soul, indeed it is to say nothing, for the two souls would not be different even if they were variously changed. It will be better to say that a rational creature's substantial form is created, but a certain brute substantial form belongs to man, which is no more the form of man than the form of a hand is the form of man. If one says that the souls of beasts are also created every day by God, then it is to be feared that someone might infer that it is therefore equally probable that they may also in turn be annihilated every day by God, when the animal dies. If this annihilation is so ordinary and frequent then it destroys all reasoning for the immortality of the human soul that is drawn from the fact that this soul cannot perish except by annihilation.

2. Souls are either created every day or are coeval with the world (summer 1683–winter 1684/1685?)[3]

If souls had a natural origin then they could also be extinguished naturally, for nothing is more agreeable to reason than that each thing can be dissolved and removed in the same way as it was bound together and constituted. And so it must be said that souls cannot arise except by creation, i.e. by a miracle, just as their immortality does not protect them from being destroyed by annihilation, i.e. by a miracle, if God willed it. And hence souls are either created every day, or, which I would prefer, are coeval with the world.

3. On the creation of souls and the origin of minds (summer 1683–winter 1684/1685?)[4]

It must be said that souls are either created every day by God, or that they pre-existed from the beginning of the world having been created once, and they lay hidden in seeds until, when the organs have been formed, the power was given to reveal themselves. It seems that it is not sufficiently agreeable to reason to speak first about the souls of beasts, and second about the human soul. For if the souls of beasts are created and infused by God, everything will be full of miracles, or special operations, which I think is not sufficiently probable. But if we suggest that human souls are likewise created in the beginning by God to lie hidden in seeds and await conception, we fall into another paradox, because evidently innumerable human souls may remain unused in seeds and never come to use reason. But if someone were to say that the soul which lies hidden even in the seeds of man is irrational, and eventually is made rational when the organs have been formed, he will be compelled to say that the irrational and rational soul differ not in kind but by organs, which is even more intolerable. But if someone were to say that only human souls are created at the time of conception, he makes human seeds inferior to the seeds of beasts, for who would believe that souls are rather inside the seeds or eggs of animals, but no souls are in humans alone? Shall we therefore say that there is in man a kind of irrational or sensitive soul, which is in the seed, but the rational soul is infused by God upon conception? But this is thought contrary to the definition of a certain council,[5] and in fact there is only one form of one body. But if, therefore, it is not to be admitted that there are two souls, one which is the mind, the other which is sensitive, because the council has defined the rational soul to be the form of the body, it remains that we say that the mind or rational soul is made from the sensitive soul at the moment of the infusion by God of a new perfection by an additional creation, or transmuted by the supernatural.

4. On the souls of men and beasts (1710?)[6]

Matter taken in itself, i.e. bare matter, is constituted from antitypy and extension. I call 'antitypy' that attribute through which matter is in space. Extension is continuation through space, or continuous diffusion through place. And so, as long as antitypy is continuously diffused or extended through place, and nothing else is assumed, there arises matter in itself, or bare matter.

The modification or variation of antitypy consists in variation of place. The modification of extension consists in variation of size and shape. From this it is obvious that matter is something merely passive, since its attributes and their variations involve no action. And insofar as we consider in motion only variation of place, of magnitude and of shape, we consider only what is merely passive.

But if we add an actual variation or an actual principle of motion, we end up with something besides bare matter. In the same way, it is obvious that perception cannot be deduced from bare matter since it consists in some action. The same thing can be understood about any kind of perception, especially in this way. If nothing were present in an organism except a machine, i.e. bare matter having variations of place, magnitude and shape, nothing could be deduced and explained from this except a mechanism, i.e. such variations as we have mentioned. For from each thing taken in itself, nothing can be deduced and explained except variations of its attributes and those of its constitutive parts.

Hence we easily conclude also that in any mill or clock taken by itself no perceiving principle is found that is produced in the thing itself; and it does not matter whether solids, fluids or a compound of both are considered in the machine. Moreover, we know that there is no essential difference between coarse and fine bodies except that of size. From this it follows that if it cannot be conceived how perception arises in a crude machine, however constructed from fluids or solids, it also cannot be conceived how perception arises from a subtler machine, for if our senses were also more subtle it would be the same as if we were perceiving a crude machine, as we do now. And so it must be considered as certain that from mechanism alone, i.e. bare matter and its modifications, perception cannot be explained any more than the principle of action and motion.

And hence it must be admitted that there is something besides matter which is both the principle of perception or of internal action, and of motion or external action. And such a principle we call substantial, likewise primitive force, primary entelechy, and in a word, soul, since the active conjoined with the passive constitutes a complete substance. But it is obvious that this principle is not extended, otherwise it would involve matter, contrary to the hypothesis. For we have shown that there is something added to bare matter. Therefore a soul will be a substantial simple thing, having no parts outside of parts. Moreover, it is a consequence of this that a primitive entelechy cannot be destroyed naturally, because every natural destruction consists in the dissolution of parts.

From this it follows either that beasts are mere machines lacking perception, as the Cartesians think, or that beasts have an indestructible soul. But because it is clear from elsewhere, namely from the nature of motion, that primitive entelechies are dispersed throughout matter and are indestructible, why should we not attribute to them not only motive action but also perception, so that they might be considered as like souls when they are joined to organic bodies? And the very analogy of things confirms it. For since in beasts everything up to perception and sensation may be considered to be just as in humans, and nature is uniform in its variety, uniform down to its principles, varied down to its modes, it is probable that there is perception in beasts also; or rather, beasts are presumed to be endowed with perception until the contrary is proved.

The Cartesians give a reason for denying perception to beasts, which is that, if we ascribe perception to beasts then we must attribute indestructible souls to them. But this conclusion, which many among them consider absurd, is not at all absurd, as we shall soon show, after a distinction between the indestructibility of the soul of beasts and the immortality of the human soul has been brought forward.

But this can also be proved by a positive and necessary argument from the fact that every primitive entelechy must have perception. For every primary entelechy has an internal variation, according to which external actions are also varied. But perception is nothing other than that very representation of external variation in internal variation. Therefore, since primitive entelechies are dispersed everywhere in matter, as can easily be shown from the fact that the principles of motion are dispersed throughout matter, it is a consequence that souls are also scattered everywhere in matter, in proportion to functioning organs; and hence the organic bodies of beasts are also endowed with souls.

Moreover, it can be understood from this that separate souls do not exist naturally, for as they are primitive or merely active entelechies they have need of some passive principle, through which they are completed.

But, you will say, an organic body can be destroyed. I answer that even if a body is destroyed according to our perception, nevertheless the soul would not for that reason be destroyed, for there would remain an animated mass and the soul would continue to act on the inside and outside, though less perfectly, i.e. without sensation. And we retain such a perception in deep sleep, apoplexy and other cases, although the senses may cease. For sensation is perception that involves something distinct and is joined with attention and memory. But a confused aggregate of many little perceptions, containing nothing eminent that excites attention, induces a stupor. Nevertheless the soul, or the power of sensing in it, would not for that reason be useless, although it would now be prevented from being exercised, because with time the mass could again develop and be adapted for sensation, so that the stupor ceases, just as more distinct perceptions arise when the body also becomes more perfect and more ordered.

And since many distinguished observers today conclude that before conception animals lie hidden in seeds in the form of insensible animalcules, so that the generation of an animal is nothing other than its unfolding and increasing, and an animal never begins naturally but is only transformed, it is therefore reasonable that just as it does not begin naturally, it does not end naturally either; thus death in turn will be nothing other than an involution and diminution of the animal, when it returns from the state of a large animal to the state of an animalcule.

Moreover, just as in us the will corresponds to the intellect, so in every primitive entelechy, appetite, or the endeavour of acting tending towards new perception, corresponds to perception. For not only is the variety of the object represented in the perceiver, but there is also a variation of the representation itself, because what is to be represented is also varied.

However, lest we are seen to make man too equal to a beast, it must be understood that there is an immense difference between the perception of men and beasts. For besides the lowest degree of perception that is found even in the stupefied (as has been explained), and a middle degree which we call sensation and recognize in beasts, there is a higher degree which we call thought. But thought is perception joined with reason, which beasts, so far as we can tell, do not have.

But because this matter has not been very well explained until now (for while some even deny sensation to beasts, others even attribute reason to them and report many cases in which beasts seem to connect certain consequences), it should be known that there are in the world two totally different sorts of inferences, empirical and rational. Empirical inferences are common to us as well as to beasts, and consist in the fact that when sensing things that have a number of times been experienced to be connected we expect them to be connected again. Thus dogs that have been beaten a number of times when they have done something displeasing expect a beating again if they do the same thing, and therefore they avoid doing it; this they have in common with infants. And a certain American thought that a letter had betrayed his crime by seeing it, because those ways of betraying which were known to him worked in this way. But because it often happens that such things are only connected by accident, empirics are often deceived by this, as are beasts, so that what they expect to happen may not happen. Thus if I give food to a dog doing something pleasing it indeed happens by accident on account of my free will; but once it has grown accustomed to the action that I wished to teach it I no longer give food to it when it acts correctly, although until that point it expects this to happen. Similarly, if some Batavian[7] boarding a ship is carried off to Asia, and brought to a Turkish city, whereupon he looks for beer in an inn like that of his home, he will be deceived in the same way, for he will expect something from the inn which is connected with it only by accident, and is not found in Turkish inns in the same way as in Batavian ones. But a man, insofar as he does not act empirically but rationally, does not rely on experience alone, or *a posteriori* inductions from particular cases, but proceeds *a priori* through reasons. And such a difference exists between a geometer, or one skilled in analysis, and someone untrained in genuine mathematics who teaches children on the basis of having committed the rules of arithmetic to memory, but does not know the reason for them, and hence cannot answer questions that are in some way different from those he is accustomed to: such is the difference between an empiric and a rational being, between the inferences of beasts and human reasoning. For even if we experience many successive examples, we are still never certain of continuous success, unless we discover necessary reasons from which we deduce that the matter cannot be otherwise. Therefore beasts (as far as we can tell) are not aware of the universality of propositions, because they are not aware of the basis of necessity. And although empirics are sometimes led by inductions to true universal propositions, nevertheless it only happens by accident, not by the force of consequence.

Finally, man is assigned by God to a much higher end, namely, to a society with him; and therefore (on account of the harmony of the kingdoms of nature and grace) it has been established that human souls are preserved together with some organic body, not only in the manner of beasts, which are perhaps stupefied for a time after death, but in a more noble way, so that they retain sensation and consciousness and are capable of punishment and reward.

B. The Relationship Between Soul and Body[8]

1. On the system of occasional causes (March 1689–March 1690?)[9]

The system of occasional causes must be partly accepted and partly rejected. Each substance is the true and real cause of its own immanent actions, and has the power of acting, and although it is sustained by the divine concourse nevertheless it cannot happen that it is merely passive, and this is true both in the case of corporeal substances and incorporeal ones. But on the other hand, each substance (excepting God alone) is nothing except the occasional cause of its transeunt actions towards another substance. Therefore the true reason of the union between soul and body, and the reason why one body adjusts itself to the state of another body, is nothing other than that the different substances of the same system of the world are created from the beginning in such a way that from the laws of their own nature they harmonize with one another.

2. New system of the nature of the communication of substances, as well as the union that exists between the soul and the body (27 June 1695)[10]

It has been several years since I conceived this system and communicated some of it to learned men, and in particular one of the greatest theologians and philosophers of our time,[11] who, having learned some of my opinions through a person of the highest rank, found them to be great paradoxes. But upon receiving my clarifications he retracted his objections in the most generous and edifying manner possible, and having approved some of my propositions he withdrew his censure of the others with which he did yet not agree. Since then I continued my meditations as and when I could, in order to give to the public only opinions that had been well examined, and I also endeavoured to answer the objections made against my essays on dynamics which have some connection with this. Finally, as some important people have desired to see my opinions further clarified, I ventured these opinions, although they are by no means popular or suitable to the taste of all sorts of mind. I am apt to do this principally to benefit from the judgement of those who are enlightened in these matters, because it would be too troublesome to seek out and ask separately all those who would be disposed to give me instruction, which I will always be delighted to receive, provided that the love of truth is evident in it rather than the passion for preconceived opinions.

Although I am one of those people who have worked much on mathematics, I have not ceased meditating on philosophy since my youth, because it seemed to me that there was a way of establishing something solid in it by clear demonstrations. I had gone far into the country of the Scholastics when mathematics and modern authors brought me out again while I was still quite young. Their beautiful ways of explaining nature mechanically charmed me, and I rightly scorned the method of those who only make use of forms or faculties, from which we learn nothing. But afterwards, having tried to go further into the very principles of mechanics, in order to explain the laws of nature that are known from experience, I realized that a consideration of an *extended mass* alone is not sufficient, and that we must also make use of the notion of *force*, which is perfectly intelligible, although it falls within the realm of metaphysics. It also seemed to me that the opinion of those who transform or degrade the beasts into pure machines, although it seems possible, is improbable, and even contrary to the order of things.

At first, when I freed myself from the yoke of Aristotle, I was seduced by the void and atoms, since they better satisfy the imagination. But returning to them after much meditation, I saw that it is impossible to find *the principles of a true unity* in matter alone, or in what is only passive, because it is only a collection or mass of parts to infinity. Now a multitude can only derive its reality from *true unities* which come from elsewhere and which are entirely different from mathematical points, which are only the extremities of extended things and modifications, and it is certain that *the continuum* could not be composed of such things. Therefore to find these *real unities*, I was compelled to have recourse to a real and animated point, so to speak, or to an atom of substance which must contain some form or activity in order to make a complete being.[12] It was therefore necessary to recall and, as it were, rehabilitate the *substantial forms*, so disparaged today, but in a way that makes them intelligible and which separates the use that should be made of them from their previous misuse. I found, therefore, that their nature consists in force, and from that force follows something analogous to sensation and appetite, and thus it was necessary to conceive them as being rather like the notion we have of *souls*. But just as the soul ought not to be made use of to explain in detail the economy of an animal's body, I likewise judged that we must not use these forms to solve particular problems of nature, although they are necessary to establish its true general principles. Aristotle calls them *first entelechies*, I call them, perhaps more intelligibly, *primitive forces*, which do not contain only the *actuality* or the fulfilment of possibility, but also an original *activity*.

I saw that these forms and souls had to be indivisible, as well as our minds, as in effect I remembered that this was St. Thomas's opinion as regards the souls of beasts. But this truth revived the great difficulties of the origin and duration of souls and forms. For as every *simple substance* which has a true unity can begin or end only by a miracle, it follows that they could only begin by creation and only end by annihilation. Thus I was obliged to recognize that (except for the souls that God still wants to create specially) the constitutive forms of substances must have been created with the world and always subsist. Thus some Scholastics, such as Albert the Great and John Bacon, had glimpsed part of the truth of their origin. And the idea should not seem extraordinary, because we are only giving to forms the duration that Gassendists grant to their atoms.

Nevertheless I judged that we must not indiscriminately mix or confuse with other forms or souls the *mind* or rational soul, which is of a superior order, and has incomparably more perfection than these forms which are sunk in matter, which in my view can be found everywhere. In comparison with those, minds or rational souls are like little Gods made in the image of God, having within them some ray of the divine light. This is why God governs minds as a Prince governs his subjects, and even as a father cares for his children; whereas he arranges other substances as an engineer handles his machines. Thus minds have special laws, which place them above the revolutions of matter by the very order that God placed in them, and it can be said that everything else is made only for them, these very revolutions being adapted to the happiness of the good and the punishment of the wicked.

However, to return to ordinary forms, or *brute souls*, this duration that we must attribute to them, instead of the one that has been attributed to atoms, might give rise to the doubt whether they do not pass from body to body, which would be *metempsychosis*, and is more or less what some philosophers have believed with regard to the transmission of motion or of species. But this fancy is very far removed from the nature of things. There is no such passage of souls, and it is here that the transformations of Mr Swammerdam, Mr Malpighi and Mr Leeuwenhoek, who are some of the best observers of our times, came to my assistance, and have allowed me to accept more easily that the animal and every other organized substance does not begin when we believe it does, and that its apparent generation is only a development, and a kind of augmentation. I have also noticed that the author of the *Search after Truth*,[13] Mr Regis, Mr Hartsoeker and other clever men, have not been far removed from this opinion.

But there still remained the most important question of what becomes of these souls or forms at the death of the animal, or at the destruction of the individual organized substance. And this question is all the more awkward inasmuch as it hardly seems reasonable that souls remain uselessly in a chaos of confused matter. Ultimately this made me think that there was only one reasonable view to take, and that is the one of the conservation not only of the soul, but also of the animal itself, and of its organic machine; although the destruction of its cruder parts has reduced it to such a small size that it escapes our senses in the same way that it did before birth. Thus there is no one who can tell the true time of death, which for a long time can pass for a simple suspension of observable actions. And death is ultimately nothing other than that in simple animals: witness the *resuscitations* of flies drowned and buried under pulverized chalk, and several similar examples which sufficiently show that there could be many other resuscitations, and in cases much further gone, if men were in a position to repair the machine. And apparently it was something approaching this idea of which the great Democritus spoke, complete atomist though he was, although Pliny made fun of it.[14] It is therefore natural that the animal, having always been living and organized (as some insightful people are beginning to recognize), will also always remain so. And because there is thus no first birth or entirely new generation of the animal, it follows that there will never be any final extinction of it either, nor complete death taken in the metaphysical sense; and that consequently, rather than the transmigration of souls, there is only a transformation of the same animal, according to how its organs are differently folded, and more or less developed.

Rational souls, however, follow much higher laws, and are exempt from everything which could make them lose the position of citizens of the society of minds, God having provided for them so well that all the changes of matter could not make them lose the moral qualities of their personality. And it can be said that everything tends not only to the perfection of the universe in general, but also of these created beings in particular, which are destined for such a degree of happiness that the universe is concerned in it in virtue of the divine goodness which is communicated to each one insofar as the sovereign wisdom can permit.

As for the ordinary course[15] of animals and other corporeal substances, whose complete extinction has until now been widely believed and whose changes depend on mechanical rules rather than moral laws, I have noted with pleasure that the ancient author of the book on *Diet*, which is attributed to Hippocrates, had caught a glimpse of the truth when he said in express terms that animals are not born and do not die, and that the things which are thought to begin and perish only appear and disappear. This was also the opinion of Parmenides, and also that of Melissus according to Aristotle.[16] For these ancients were sounder than we think.

I am as well disposed as anyone to do justice to the moderns; nevertheless I find that they have carried reform too far, amongst other things by confusing natural things with artificial, through not having sufficiently grand ideas of the majesty of nature. They hold that the difference between nature's machine and ours is only that of great to small. This recently brought a very clever man to say that, by considering nature closely, we find it less admirable than we had thought, it being only like the workshop of a craftsman.[17] I believe that this does not give a sufficiently just or worthy idea of nature, and there is only our system which ultimately shows the true and immense distance between the least productions and mechanisms of divine wisdom and the greatest masterpieces of art brought forth from a limited mind; this difference is not merely one of degree, but one of kind. We must therefore recognize that the machines of nature have a truly infinite number of organs, and are so well provided for and proofed against all accidents that it is not possible to destroy them. A natural machine still remains a machine in the least parts, and what is more, it always remains the same machine that it was, only being transformed by the different foldings that it receives, and it is sometimes extended, sometimes contracted and as it were concentrated, when we believe that it has disappeared.

Moreover, by means of the soul or form there is a true unity which answers to what is called 'I' in us, which could not occur in the machines of art or in the simple mass of matter, however organized it might be. This mass can only be regarded as like an army or a flock, or like a pond full of fish, or like a watch composed of springs and wheels. However if there were no true substantial unities, there would be nothing substantial or real in the collection. It was this that forced Mr Cordemoy to abandon Descartes by embracing the doctrine of Democritus's atoms, in order to find a true unity. But *atoms of matter* are contrary to reason; aside from the fact that they are also composed of parts, since the invincible attachment of one part to another (even if this could be conceived or reasonably supposed) would not destroy their diversity. There are only *atoms of substance*, that is to say, real unities absolutely devoid of parts, which are the sources of actions, and the absolute first principles of the composition of things, and as it were the ultimate elements of analysis of substantial things. They can be called *metaphysical points*: they have *something vital* in them, and a kind of *perception*, and *mathematical points* are their *points of view* for expressing the universe. But when corporeal substances are contracted, all their organs together make only one *physical point* as far as we are concerned. Thus physical points are only indivisible in appearance. Mathematical points are exact, but they are only modalities; it is only metaphysical points or substance (constituted by forms or souls) which are exact and real, and without them there would be nothing real, because without true unities there would be no multitude.

After establishing these things, I thought I had reached port, but when I set myself to meditate on the union of the soul with the body I was as it were thrown back onto the open sea. For I could not find any means of explaining how the body makes something pass into the soul, or vice versa, nor how one substance can communicate with another created substance. Mr Descartes left the game at that point, insofar as one can tell from his writings. But his disciples, seeing that the common opinion is inconceivable, thought that we sense the qualities of bodies because God arouses thoughts in the soul on the occasion of the motions of matter, and when our soul in its turn wants to move the body, they thought that it is God who moves the body for it. And as the communication of motions appeared to them to be inconceivable, they believed that God gives motion to a body on the occasion of the motion of another body. This is what they call the *system of occasional causes*, which has been very much in fashion because of the fine reflections of the author of the *Search after Truth*.

It must be acknowledged that this has gone a fair way into the difficulty, in explaining what cannot be the case; but their explanation of what really happens does not appear to have removed the difficulty. It is quite true that there is no real influence, in the strict metaphysical sense, of one created substance on another, and that all things, with all their realities, are continually produced by the power of God: but to resolve the problems, it is not enough to make use of the general cause and to bring in what is called *Deus ex machina*. For when this is done without there being any other explanation drawn from the order of secondary causes, it is in fact to have recourse to a miracle. In philosophy we must endeavour to explain by showing the way in which things are carried out by the divine wisdom, in accordance with the notion of the subject in question.

Being therefore obliged to grant that it is not possible that the soul or some other true substance could receive something from outside, except through divine omnipotence, I was led insensibly to a thought that surprised me, but which appears inevitable, and which in effect has some very great advantages and considerable beauty. Namely, that we should therefore say that God first created the soul, or any other real unity of such sort, so that everything must arise in it from its own nature, by a perfect *spontaneity* with regard to itself, and yet with a perfect *conformity* to things outside it. And thus our internal sensations (that is to say, those which are in the soul itself, and not in the brain or in the subtle parts of the body) being only phenomena following external beings, or rather true appearances and as it were well-ordered dreams, it must be the case that these internal perceptions in the soul itself come about through its own original constitution, that is to say through the representative nature (capable of expressing beings outside it in relation to its organs) which it was given at its creation and which constitutes its individual character. And this is what makes each of these substances represent accurately the whole universe in its way and according to a certain point of view, and makes the perceptions and expressions of external things occur in the soul at the right moment in virtue of its own laws, just as in a world apart, and just as if nothing existed beyond God and that soul (to make use of a manner of speaking used by a certain person who had an exalted mind, and whose holiness is famous), there will be a perfect agreement between all these substances, which gives rise to the same effect that would be noticed if they communicated with each other through a transmission of species or qualities, as ordinary philosophers believe. Moreover, the organized mass in which lies the soul's point of view, is expressed more immediately by it, and finds itself reciprocally ready to act of itself, following the laws of the corporeal machine, in the moment that the soul wills it, without one disturbing the laws of the other, the spirits and the blood having exactly at that time the motions that are needed to correspond to the passions and the perceptions of the soul. It is this mutual relationship, arranged in advance in each substance of the universe, which produces what we call their communication, and which alone constitutes *the union of the soul and the body.* And from that it can be understood how the soul has its seat in the body by an immediate presence, which could not be greater because the soul is in the body in the same way as unity is in the result of unities which is a multitude.

This hypothesis is perfectly possible. For why could God not initially give to a substance a nature or internal force which could produce in it in an orderly way (as in a *spiritual or formal automaton, but free* in the case of one which has received reason) everything that will happen to it, that is to say, all the appearances or expressions that it will have, and all that without the assistance of any created thing? It is all the more probable since the nature of substance necessarily requires and essentially contains a progress or a change, without which it would not have any force to act. And this nature of the soul is representative of the universe in a very exact way (although more or less distinct), the series of representations that the soul produces in itself will naturally correspond to the series of changes in the universe itself; just as, on the other hand, the body has been accommodated to the soul for the confluences in which it is conceived as acting outside itself. What is all the more reasonable is that bodies are made only for minds capable of entering into society with God, and of celebrating his glory. Thus as soon as we see the possibility of this *hypothesis of agreements,* we also see that it is the most reasonable, and that it gives a wonderful idea of the harmony of the universe and of the perfection of God's works.

It also has this great advantage, in that instead of saying that we are free only in appearance and in a way sufficient for practice, as some clever people have believed, we should rather say that we are determined only in appearance, and that in strict metaphysical terms we are perfectly independent of the influence of all other created things. This again puts the immortality of the soul in a wonderful light, as well as the forever uniform conservation of our individuality, perfectly well ordered by its own nature, sheltered from all external accidents, whatever the appearances to the contrary. Never has a system made our elevated position so evident. Every mind is like a world apart, sufficient unto itself, independent of every other created thing. It contains the infinite, expresses the universe; it is as durable, as subsistent, as the universe of created things itself. We should therefore hold that every mind should play its part in the manner most appropriate to contribute to the perfection of the society of all minds, which constitutes their moral union in the City of God. We also find here a new proof of the existence of God, which is extraordinarily clear. For this perfect agreement of so many substances, which have no communication with one another at all, could come only from a common cause.

Besides all these advantages, which make this hypothesis recommendable, it can be said that it is something more than a hypothesis, because it scarcely appears possible to explain things in any other intelligible way, and that several great difficulties which have exercised men's minds until now seem to disappear of themselves when it is properly understood. It also preserves our ordinary manners of speaking. For it can be said that the substance whose disposition explains change in an intelligible way, so that it can be thought that it is to this substance that others have been accommodated in this respect from the beginning, in accordance with the order of God's decrees, is the one that must be conceived in that respect as *acting* upon the others. Also the action of one substance on another is not an emission or transplantation of an entity as is commonly thought, and it could be reasonably taken only in the way that I have just said. It is true that we can very well conceive matter as emitting and receiving parts, by which we are right to explain mechanically all the phenomena of physics; but as a material mass is not a substance, it is evident that action in regard to substance itself could only be that which I have just said.

These considerations, however metaphysical they may seem, are still wonderfully useful in physics in order to establish the laws of motion, as our dynamics will be able to show. For it can be said that in the collision of bodies each suffers only from its own elasticity, caused by the motion which is already in it. And as for absolute motion, nothing can determine it mathematically, since everything ends in relations. This ensures that there is always a perfect equivalence of hypotheses, as in astronomy, so that whatever number of bodies we take, it is arbitrary to assign rest or even such and such a degree of speed to whichever one we choose without the phenomena of straight, circular or composite motion being able to refute it. However it is reasonable to attribute true motion to bodies in accordance with the supposition which explains phenomena in the most intelligible way, this denomination being in accordance with the notion of action that we have just established.

3. Clarification of the 'New system of the communication of substances', serving as a response to what was said about it in the Journal on 12 September 1695 (3 January 1696)[18]

I see clearly from your remarks that my thoughts, which were placed in the *Journal des Savants*, need some clarification. You say that you do not know, Sir, how I could prove what I have put forward concerning the communication or harmony of two substances as different as the soul and the body. It is true that I believed I had given the way to do it. And here is how I hope to satisfy you.

Imagine two clocks or watches which perfectly agree. Now this could happen *in three ways*. *The first* consists in a natural influence. This is what Mr Huygens experienced to his great surprise. He had suspended two pendulums from the same piece of wood; the continual strokes of the pendulums communicated similar vibrations to the particles of wood, but as these vibrations could not keep their order without interfering with each other, unless the pendulums were in agreement, it happened by a kind of miracle that even when their strokes were disturbed on purpose they returned to swinging together, rather like two strings which are in unison. *The second way* to make two clocks always agree, even bad ones, would be to have them forever managed by a skilful worker who sets them right and then keeps them in agreement at each moment. *The third way* is to make these two clocks from the start with such skill and accuracy that we could be certain of their agreement from then on.

Now suppose the soul and the body in the place of these two watches; their agreement or sympathy will also happen by one of these three ways. *The way of influence* is the one of ordinary philosophy, but as we cannot conceive either material particles or kinds of immaterial species or qualities which can pass from one of these substances into the other, we are obliged to abandon this view. *The way of assistance* is the one of occasional causes. But I hold that this is to invoke a *Deus ex machina* in a natural and ordinary thing, where according to reason God should only intervene in the way that he concurs with all other natural things. Thus there remains only my hypothesis, that is to say *the way of the harmony pre-established* by an anticipatory divine artifice, which has formed from the beginning each of these substances so that by only following its own laws which it received with its being it nevertheless agrees with the other, just as if there were a mutual influence, or as if God always had a hand in it beyond his general concourse. After that, I do not believe that I need to prove anything, unless someone wants me to prove that God is skilful enough to be able to make use of this anticipatory artifice, of which we see examples even among men, in proportion to their skill. And supposing that he is able to do it, it is clear that it is the finest way and the one most worthy of him. You had some suspicion that my explanation would be opposed to the different ideas we have of the mind and the body. But now you clearly see, Sir, that no one has better established their independence. For while people have been obliged to explain their communication by way of a miracle, there was always the fear, which many people had, that the distinction between soul and body was not such as was believed, since it was necessary to go to such lengths to support it. Now all these scruples cease. My essays on dynamics have some relation with this; in those, it was necessary to go further into the notion of corporeal substance, which I think consists in the force of acting and resisting rather than in extension, which is only a repetition or diffusion of something anterior, that is to say, a repetition or diffusion of this force. And as these thoughts that appeared paradoxical to some led me to exchange letters with several famous people, I could show you a *commercium epistolicum* [an exchange of letters] on the matter, which would include my correspondence with Mr Arnauld, of which I spoke in my previous letter. In it there will be a curious mix of philosophical and mathematical thoughts, which will perhaps have in places the charm of novelty. I leave you to judge, Sir, if the explanations that I have just given could be suitable for sounding out the opinions of enlightened people through the medium of your Journal, but without naming me though, just as I was not named in the *Journal des Savants* either.

C. The Fate of Souls[19]

1. Letter to Electress Sophie (4 November 1696)[20]

My fundamental meditations turn on two things, namely on unity and on infinity. Souls are unities and bodies are multitudes, but infinite ones, so that the slightest grain of dust contains a world of an infinity of creatures. And microscopes have revealed even more than a million living animals in a drop of water. But unities, even though they are indivisible and without parts, nevertheless represent the multitudes, in much the same way as all the lines from the circumference are united in the centre of the circle, which alone faces it from all sides even though it does not have any size at all. The admirable nature of the sentiment consists in this reunion of infinity in the unity, which also makes each soul like a world apart, representing the larger world in its way and according to its point of view, and that consequently each soul, once it begins to exist, must be as durable as the world itself, of which it is the perpetual mirror. These mirrors are likewise universal, and each soul exactly expresses the universe in its entirety, because there is nothing in the world that does not experience the effect of everything else, although the effect may be less noticeable depending on the distance. But of all souls there are none more elevated than those that are capable of understanding the eternal truths, and not just of representing the universe in a confused manner, but also of understanding it and of having distinct ideas of the beauty and grandeur of the sovereign substance. That is, those that are capable of being the mirror not only of the universe (as all souls are), but also of what is best in the universe, that is, of God himself; and this is what is reserved for minds or intelligences, and makes them capable of governing other creatures in imitation of the creator.

Therefore, as every soul faithfully represents the whole universe, and as every mind also represents God himself in the universe, it is easy to see that minds are something greater than one thinks. For it is a certain truth that every substance must attain all the perfection of which it is capable, and that already exists enveloped within it, rather like in the way that has been discovered in our time. It is also good to consider that in this sensible life we grow old after having matured, because we approach death, which is only a change of theatre; but the perpetual life of actual souls, being exempt from death, must also be exempt from old age. That is why souls advance and ripen continually like the world itself, of which they are images. For there being nothing outside the universe, and consequently nothing that is able to hinder it, it must be that the universe advances without interruption, and develops with all the regularity possible.

One will be able to object that this universal advancement of things is not apparent, and that it even seems that there is some disorder which instead makes it go into reverse, so to speak. But this is only in appearance; we see that through the example of astronomy. The movement of the planets appeared to be a confused matter to us who are on the globe of the Earth. It seems that these stars are wandering and that they move without any rule, because they sometimes move forwards and afterwards they move backwards, and they even nearly stand still from time to time. But when, with Copernicus, we placed ourselves in the sun, at least with the mind's eye, we discovered a wonderful order. Therefore not only does everything proceed by order, but even our minds must notice it more and more as they make progress . . .

I hope that in France they will come back little by little from the mechanical sect, and from those faint notions that people have of the limited generosity of nature, as if she only granted to us the privilege of having souls. Those who have come up with that very much wanted to flatter themselves or others. And when people have a better understanding of the thoughts that they ought to have on infinity, they will have a wholly different idea of the majesty of nature than that of believing that it is simply nothing but machines, and that it is nothing greater than the shop of a workman, as the otherwise clever author of the *Conversation on the Plurality of Worlds* believed,[21] while speaking with his Marchioness. The machines of nature are infinitely above ours. For besides the fact that they have sensation, each contains an infinity of organs, and what is even more wonderful, it is for that reason that every animal is resistant to all accidents, and can never be destroyed, but only changed and strengthened by death, just like a snake sheds its old skin. Even with regard to sensible life, an animal could be resuscitated if its organs could be put right, just as in the drowned flies that I took pleasure, being a small boy, to bring back to life. But absolutely speaking, birth and death are only developments and envelopments in order to obtain a new nourishment, and to leave it afterwards, after having taken the quintessence from it, and above all after having received in itself in its way the traces of sensible perceptions, which always remain and are never erased by a complete forgetfulness. And although one does not always have the opportunity to remember them, these ideas will not fail to come back at the right moment and be useful in the course of time. It can also be demonstrated mathematically that every action, however small it might be, spreads to infinity as much with regard to places as with regard to times, radiating so to speak throughout the entire universe, and being preserved for all eternity. Thus it is not only souls but also the actions of souls which are always preserved, and even the action of each soul is preserved in each soul because of the conspiracy and sympathy of all things, the world being fully complete in each of its parts, albeit more distinctly in some than in others. And it is in this that consists the advantage of minds, for which the sovereign intelligence has made everything else, so as to make itself known and loved, multiplying itself so to speak in all these living mirrors that represent it.

2. Letter to Electress Sophie (6 February 1706)[22]

Your Electoral Highness asks me what a simple substance is. I reply that its nature is to have perception, and consequently to represent composite things.

It will be asked how the composite can be represented in the simple, or the multitude in unity. I answer that it is more or less like when an infinity of radii converge and make angles in the centre, completely simple and indivisible though this centre is.

And these radii do not merely consist in lines, but also in tendencies and efforts along the lines, which intersect without merging with each other, as we can see from the movement of fluids.

It is like when we throw several stones into still water at the same time and see that each makes circles on the surface of the water, which intersect without merging, each row of circles advancing as if it were all alone. We also see that rays of light penetrate each other without mixing. Finally, it is known that the same body can receive an infinity of impressions all at once, each of which has its effect; and the least part of a mass which is compressed and full of efforts resists the efforts of all the other parts, and this cannot occur without its receiving some impression from them. This makes me think that the actual unities from which everything else results must be modified in relation to everything that surrounds them; and it is this that constitutes the representation which is attributed to them.

God is himself a simple substance, but as he is the original and universal centre which includes and produces everything, he is of a different order. The other simple substances are what are called *souls*, and the whole of nature is full of them.

Each *soul* is a world in miniature, representing things from the outside according to its point of view, and confusedly or distinctly according to the organs which accompany it, whereas God includes everything distinctly and eminently.

Thus by using souls as so many mirrors, the author of things has found a way to multiply the very universe, so to speak, which is to say he found a way of varying the views of it: just as the same town appears differently according to the different places from which one looks at it.

And with each soul being a mirror of the universe in its way, it is easy to judge that each soul is as imperishable and incorruptible as the universe itself.

Since it can be said, moreover, that the soul is a simple substance or unity, which has no parts, it could not be formed by the composition of any parts nor destroyed by their dissolution. Souls are unities, and bodies are multitudes.

With the universe being a kind of fluid, all of one piece and like an ocean without limit, all motions within it are conserved and propagated to infinity, though insensibly, just like the circles of which I have spoken (which came about by a stone thrown in water) are propagated visibly for some distance, and although they become invisible in the end, the impression does not cease spreading itself to infinity, as is quite clear from the laws of motion.

This communication of motions means that everything is related to and affected by everything else, although more often than not distant things do not have noticeable effects.

Nevertheless, light, sound, the magnet, and some other examples prove that there are sometimes noticeable actions at a distance.

Therefore, as our organs are affected by neighbouring bodies, and those bodies by their neighbours, we are affected mediately by all other bodies; our souls too, since they represent bodies according to their organs.

It can also be inferred from that that the soul is never entirely deprived of an organic body. For order requires that every substance always relate to everything else; there is even a demonstration for this.

It follows from this that not only the soul but also the animal subsists always. Also, nature never proceeds by leaps, and does not pass from one kind to another.

Through observations it now seems quite clear that the apparent generation of a new plant or animal is only a growth and transformation of a plant or animal that already subsists in seeds.

Besides what Mr Swammerdam, Mr Leeuwenhoek and Mr Dodart have observed on this matter, it can be said that reason as well as experience leads us to this conclusion, since there is no mechanism that could draw from a shapeless mass a body endowed with an infinite number of organs, such as is that of an animal. Thus (excepting a miracle) there must necessarily be a preformation, that is to say a formation in advance. But after having recognized that the animal only comes into being at the same time as does the world, and that it only changes and develops by generation, I am surprised that it has not also been recognized that it must endure as long as the world, and that death is only a diminution and envelopment of the animal.

From all this it also seems that, as each soul is a mirror of the universe, it must follow its course just like the very universe that it represents, and that this regular course of a soul can never be completely interrupted by death, which is only a sleep (that is to say a state in which perceptions are more confused, and which lasts until they redevelop).

And just as there are grounds to think that the universe itself develops more and more, and that everything tends towards some goal (since everything comes from an author whose wisdom is perfect) it can likewise be believed that souls, which endure as long as the universe, also proceed to get better and better (at least physically), and that their perfections carry on growing; although more often than not this happens only insensibly, and sometimes after large steps backwards.

It is often necessary to move back for a better jump: death and sufferings would not exist in the universe if they were not necessary for great changes for the better. Just as a grain of corn seems to perish in the earth in order to be able to push up a shoot.

And just as there are two sorts of perception, one simple, the other accompanied by reflections that give rise to knowledge and reasoning, so there are two kinds of souls, namely ordinary souls, whose perception is without reflection, and rational souls, which think about what they do: the first are merely mirrors of the universe, but the second are also imitations of the divinity.

Ordinary souls are governed purely by examples from the senses, like empirics; but rational souls examine by reason (when they can) whether past examples are applicable to the present case. The souls of beasts consequently can never arrive at necessary and general truths; just as an empiric can never be sure if what has often been successful for him in the past (without his knowing the reason for it) will be successful for him again in the future.

It ought to be believed that there are rational souls more perfect than us, that could be called *genies*, and we could well be of their number one day. The order of the universe seems to require this.

And as the rational soul possesses reflection, which is to say that it presently thinks of itself and knows itself, it is appropriate that it should always know itself, at least when waking from sleep or emerging from some other distraction that could interrupt its attention.

Thus it is not only physically the same soul that always exists, but also the same individual *morally*; this renders it susceptible of punishments and rewards under the most perfect government, which is that of God.

Thus the best conclusion that can be drawn from the true knowledge of principles is the importance of the practice of virtue.

It is true that souls born good, or accustomed to it from early on, practise it without deliberation as they find pleasure in it. But as not everyone has this advantage, and custom and passions often lead elsewhere, it is important that one has good principles established to which even those who have received or taken to contrary inclinations can intrinsically adapt themselves little by little, and to which they can naturally return by a carefully chosen and regulated practice, if they want to make the effort with them. For one can change even one's temperament.

Besides, with good inclination joined to reason, the action is rendered more noble and more constant; for it is good and satisfying to know that one acts in accordance with reason: nothing is further removed from the beast state, and nothing approaches divinity more closely. The divine rays of goodness and wisdom shine with such brilliance in some distinguished persons with whom I have and have had the honour to have commerce (and I do not dare to name you among them, Madam, for fear of it passing for flattery), that they can serve as an example to human kind.

I am with devotion, etc.

P.S. I forgot to add that only nature in fact receives all impressions and makes one of them, but as it lacks a soul the order of the impressions matter has received cannot be disentangled, and the impressions would only be confused. Each assignable point of matter has a different motion from all the other assignable points, and its motion is composed of all preceding impressions; but this impression is as simple as those which compose it, and no composition can be recognized in it. Nevertheless, as the entire effect must always express its cause, there must be something other than matter. And where the preceding impressions are distinguished and preserved, this is where there is a soul: thus there is soul everywhere. It is true and very noteworthy that, as the soul is joined to this point of matter surrounding it, there is a way of disentangling the past. For all the impressions can be traced, so to speak, in the infinite varieties of shapes and motions that there are in that matter, which preserve something of all preceding effects. And it is also for this reason that every soul is accompanied by an organic body that corresponds to it.

Notes

1 See also II.C.2.
2 A VI iv 1495. Latin.
3 A VI iv 1494. Latin.
4 A VI iv 1496–7. Latin.
5 The Fifth Lateran Council (1512–17).
6 G VII 328–32. Latin.
7 An inhabitant of Batavia, now Holland.
8 See also I.B.3.
9 A VI iv 1640–1. Latin.
10 G IV 477–87. French. Originally published in the *Journal des Savants*.
11 In a (post-publication) revision of his own manuscript, Leibniz wrote here: 'Mr Arnauld'.
12 In a (post-publication) revision of his own manuscript, Leibniz replaced the sentence 'Therefore . . . complete being' with this: 'Now a multitude can derive its reality only from true unities which come from elsewhere and are completely different from points, from which it is certain that the continuum cannot be composed. Therefore to find the real unities I was forced to have recourse to a formal atom, because a material being cannot be at the same time material and perfectly indivisible, or endowed with a true unity.'
13 Nicolas Malebranche.
14 Pliny, *Natural History*, book VII, chapter 55.
15 Reading *cours* (Erdman) instead of *corps* (Gerhardt).
16 ACW 298b15–17.
17 In a (post-publication) revision of his own manuscript, Leibniz added here: 'author of *Conversations on the Plurality of Worlds*'. The reference is to Bernard le Bovier de Fontenelle.

18 G VI 498–500. French.
19 See also II.A.4.
20 A I xiii 90–3. French.
21 Bernard le Bovier de Fontenelle.
22 G VII 566–70. French.

III. FREE WILL AND NECESSITY

A. The Nature of Free Will

1. On free will (summer 1678–winter 1680/1681?)[1]

The question of whether we have a free will, and what its extent is, is one of the most ancient and most problematic in the world. Entire nations, and sects of ancient philosophers as well as sects of modern Christians, have taken sides on it. It is of great importance for the conduct of life; people have got into trouble because of this matter, and after that it would appear reckless to say that it is easy to resolve. I admit that it will never be settled while men amuse themselves in doubts, and seek to maintain these doubts by empty, albeit pretty speculations, rather than to end them by solid, albeit more rigorous reasonings.

The cause of the majority of endless disputes comes in part from the fact that people want to have the freedom to play with notions, and that it is believed that it would be a kind of slavery to bind oneself to firm thoughts and to fixed and well-settled ideas. Be that as it may, let us endeavour to discover the true notion of free will, and then we will see if it is something which men are capable of having.

Firstly, I suppose that men take free will for a perfection, since they attribute it to God and angels and deny it to beasts.

Secondly, I suppose that free will is contrary to constraint, which is why if someone is pulled into a house by force then it cannot be said that he went there freely. But when those who are caught at sea during a storm throw their goods overboard in order to make the ship lighter and to save themselves, it can be doubted whether they act freely. And I answer that they do, because they are not forced to save themselves if they do not want to do so.

In the third place, I suppose that free will is contrary not only to constraint but also to ignorance or error, for example when guardians do not want to give to a young man the knowledge of his belongings, it could be said that he is refused the free administration of his possessions, although they have been placed in his hands.

Hence I draw these conclusions: the more a man is powerful, in not being easily carried away by some external force, the freer he is. If a man could be powerful enough to stop in the air in the middle of a fall without any support, notwithstanding the heaviness that brings bodies towards the earth, he would doubtless be freer than ordinary men. That is why on this point the birds are freer than men, or at least men would be freer than they are if they also had the advantages of birds.

The more a man knows, the freer he is, since error and constraint are equally contrary to freedom of action, by the aforesaid suppositions.

The will is an effort that one makes to act, because one has found it good. From which it follows that one never fails to act when one wills to and when one is able to at the time. For when one makes the effort, the action itself follows necessarily from it, assuming there is nothing preventing it, that is to say, when one is able. It is therefore an axiom of the firmest and most certain kind that from the will and the power the action never fails to follow.

Hence it follows that we are the masters of our actions, that is, that we do everything that we will, so long as it does not surpass our powers. And consequently we have a complete freedom in these matters to do what seems good to us.

That is why there are no grounds to doubt our freedom in proportion to our powers and our knowledge, if we are content with what is reasonable, given that God gave us our reason to examine good and evil, and to choose between them, and then the power to act according to this choice.

But we demand something further; we are not content with the freedom to act, but also claim a freedom to will what we would will to will, which is a contradictory thing, and would be dangerous if it were possible. It will be easy to demonstrate both of these points.

I therefore say that the freedom to will everything that one would will is an impossible thing. For if it were possible, it would proceed to infinity; for example, if someone asked me why I will something, and if I responded 'because I will to will', he would have the same right to ask me for the reason of this second will, and if I always resorted to a new will to will, the matter would never have an end, and there would have to be wills to will infinite in number preceding the will to act, or rather we would finally have to come to a reason for willing which is not taken from the will but the understanding; for we do not will because we will to will, but because our nature is to will what we believe to be the best. And this belief does not come from our will but from the nature of things, or from the state of our mind. All we can do about that is make use of all the suitable means to think well, so that things appear to us according to their nature rather than according to our prejudices.

Therefore there is no freedom of indifference, as it is called in the Schools. For the freedom to will that many claim, and that they say consists in indifference, such that we can suspend action and will without any reason that moves us to it, is not only an impossible thing, since every created being has some cause, but also useless, and something which would even be dangerous; so much so that we would not be liable to thank nature if it had given us so irrational a faculty.

It is also contrary to the suppositions which were made at the start, and which are in keeping with good sense, because freedom must be a perfection, yet this indifference, or this faculty of rejecting the best without any reason, true or apparent, is rather indicative of a great imperfection; and it does not exist either in God or in the angels confirmed in the good. Therefore true freedom of the mind consists in recognizing and choosing the best; and as we established above, that one is freer the more knowledge one has, this is completely the opposite with regard to indifference, which is rather a result of ignorance, since the more one is educated, the less one will be indifferent or uncertain about the choice that one has to make; and the more one is accustomed to following reason, the more determined one will be to carry out what one judges the most reasonable.

I therefore conclude that true freedom consists in the power that we have to reason carefully about things and to act according to what we have judged the best. And the more we use reason in things which are not beyond our powers, the more free will we have; but as our reasonings have some connection with the movements of the body, which change according to external impressions, it often happens that sudden encounters, great passions, prejudices and customs ingrained and traced in the brain, and lastly diseases, make us will and act before we have reasoned. Consequently our free will is mingled with some constraint. But the more a man will accustom himself to not rushing into things, which is called firmness of mind, the more he will be free.

2. On freedom and spontaneity (after 1690)[2]

Freedom is spontaneity joined to intelligence.

Thus what is called spontaneity in beasts and other substances lacking in intelligence, is elevated in man to a higher degree of perfection, and is called freedom.

Spontaneity is contingency without compulsion, or rather, we call spontaneous that which is neither necessary nor constrained.

We call *contingent* what is not necessary, or (what is the same thing) that whose opposite is possible, implying no contradiction.

Constrained is where the principle comes from the outside.

There is indifference when there is no more reason for one thing than for another. Without that there would be determination.

All actions of individual substances are contingent. For it can be shown that in cases where things could have happened otherwise, there would be no contradiction as a result.

All actions are determined and never indifferent. For there is always a reason that inclines us towards one action rather than another, since nothing happens without a reason. It is true that these inclining reasons are not necessitating, and destroy neither contingency nor freedom.

A freedom of indifference is impossible. So much so that it cannot be found anywhere, not even in God. For God is determined by himself to always do the best. And creatures are always determined by internal or external reasons.

The more substances are determined by themselves, and removed from indifference, the more perfect they are. For always being determined, they will have the determination either from themselves, and will be so much the more powerful and perfect, or they will have it from the outside, and then they will be proportionally obliged to serve external things.

The more we act according to reason, the freer we are, and there is so much more servitude the more we act in accordance with the passions. For the more we act according to reason, the more we act according to the perfections of our own nature, and insofar as we allow ourselves to be carried away by passions, we are slaves to external things, which act upon us.

In summary: all actions are contingent, or without necessity. But also everything is determined or ordered, and there is no indifference at all. It can even be said that substances are all the more free when they are removed from indifference and determined by themselves. And the more they approach the divine perfection the less need they have to be determined from the outside. For God, being the most free and most perfect substance, is also the most determined by himself to do the most perfect. But the more one is ignorant and impotent, the more one is indifferent. So much so that nothingness, which is most imperfect and furthest removed from God, is also the most indifferent and the least determined. Now insofar as we have wisdom and act in accordance with reason, to that extent we will be determined by the perfections of our own nature, and consequently we will be all the more free as we will have fewer hindrances to our choice. It is true that all our perfections and those of all nature come from God, but far from this being contrary to freedom it is rather on account of it that we are free, because God communicated to us a degree of his perfection and of his freedom. Let us therefore be content with a freedom which is desirable and approaches that of God, which makes us most inclined to choose good and to do good, and not lay claim to a harmful, not to mention fanciful freedom of being in uncertainty and a perpetual predicament, like this ass of Buridan, famous in the Schools, who, being placed at an equal distance between two bags of oats, and having nothing to determine him to go to one rather than to the other, let himself die of hunger.

3. Conversation about freedom and fate (1699–1703?)[3]

Sir,

Since you asked me whether I had anything put in writing on the subject which so dominated our last conversation, I thought it would not upset you to see a part of it here, even though it will contain more, and also less, than a full version would.

It has always seemed to me that the questions about freedom and fate and those that are related to them, are all empty, and that people make them more difficult than they are. In order to see this, it is important to properly clarify the terms, and to make the right oppositions: therefore we have to oppose necessity to contingency, determination to indifference, spontaneity to impulse, the voluntary to the undeliberate, and freedom to bondage.

Necessary is that whose opposite or *not being* is impossible or implies a contradiction, or rather *necessary* is that which could not not-exist;[4] and contingent is that which can not-exist, or where its not-being does not imply any contradiction. Consequently the whole universe and everything in it is contingent and could be otherwise. But if a single manner of the universe was possible, or rather if everything possible happened, the universe would be necessary; and this is the opinion of Hobbes, of Spinoza, of some ancients, and perhaps of Mr Descartes.[5] But as it is not credible, or even possible, that all stories occur together and become true histories in some world, we must conclude from that, and from quite a few reasons, that the world or the universe could be made in an infinity of ways, and that God has chosen the best of those. That is why, absolutely speaking, every matter of fact, the whole world and everything that happens in it, is contingent, and we can say that all the things of the world exist without absolute necessity, but they do not exist without hypothetical necessity or the necessity of connection. For once God has chosen this arrangement, and foreseen or rather arranged everything in advance, it can be said that, with this assumed, everything is necessary hypothetically or following this supposition; and this is what theologians and philosophers agree upon, distinguishing between an absolute necessity (which is not the case here) and a necessity of supposition or of the hypothesis, which cannot be denied once foreknowledge or providence and the completely determined order of things is granted.

But even if there is no absolute necessity in passing things, we must always acknowledge that everything is absolutely certain and *determined* in them. And the determination is not a necessity, but an inclination that is always greater towards what happens than towards what does not happen, so that it can be said that the same relation exists between the necessity and the inclination as there is in the analysis of mathematicians between an exact equation and the limits which give an approximation. For although this world is not at all necessary, because there are other ways which do not imply a contradiction, nevertheless God does nothing but follow the most perfect reason and has been determined by that to choose it. And what is more, every cause in the world has been determined to produce such-and-such an effect under such-and-such circumstances, and even we are determined to take the side for which the balance of the deliberation in which enter true or false reasons, as well as the passions, makes us lean towards the most. And when this happens our action is voluntary, otherwise it is *undeliberated*. Thus although these determinations do not strictly speaking *necessitate*, they do not fail to *incline*, and we always follow the side where there is the greatest inclination or disposition:

because the case of a perfect indifference, which is that of Buridan's ass between two meadows which allows itself to die, is imaginary, because the perfect equality of one side with the other can never take place. Otherwise it would have to be the case that the universe, which gives impulses to everything, was also equally divided and made in a similar manner, one part equivalent to or balanced against another, just as the circle is equally divided by its diameter or the square by its diagonal, which could not be.

Therefore the Christian Schools and especially the Thomists, after their leader, were justified in maintaining that the truth of future contingents is determined. This is nothing other than their applying the general rule of contradiction, which is the principle of all our universal knowledge, namely that every intelligible statement is either true or false, whether it is the present and the past being spoken of, or the future; although we do not always know on which side the truth is. And people have mocked, with the ancients, the good-natured Epicurus, man of intellect but clearly ignorant, who, when he had to talk about some profound matter, feared fate, and wanted that statement which can be made about the future to be neither true nor false,[6] as if the future is not just as certainly future as the past is certainly past, whether one knows the one and the other or does not know it. Not to mention now what Epicurus did not accept, namely that the future is always known by God.

Thus although we act with *spontaneity,* in that there is a principle of action within us, and we are not without life and do not need to be pushed like puppets, and although our spontaneity is conjoined with knowledge and deliberation or choice, which makes our actions *voluntary,* nevertheless we must acknowledge that we are always predetermined, and that apart from our previous inclinations or dispositions, new impressions from objects also contribute to incline us, and all these inclinations joined together and balanced against the contrary inclinations never fail to form a general prevalent inclination. For as we are dependent on the universe, and as we act in it, it must be the case that we are also acted upon. We determine ourselves, and are free insofar as we act, and we are determined by external things and as it were subject to them insofar as we are acted upon. But in one way or another we are always determined on the inside or from the outside, which is to say, more inclined to what happens or will happen than to what will not happen.

And so far from indetermination or absolute indifference (without any prevailing inclination, if it were possible) being a privilege, it is rather an absurdity, and indetermination in itself is an imperfection that we should not claim. Even God, who is the most perfect, is also the most determined to act in a manner conforming to supreme reason, and the apparent indetermination or equality of the balance, in which we sometimes find ourselves, comes from ignorance or impotence, and nevertheless is never exactly a true indetermination when we make a resolution, although another ignorance, which is to say that of an infinity of small influences upon us of which we are not aware, makes it seem so. This shows that it is always very true that our *freedom*, and that of all other intelligent substances up to God himself, is accompanied by a certain degree of indifference or contingency, which has been defined so that we and those other substances are never necessitated, because the opposite of what is done is always possible or does not imply any contradiction. But as there is always more inclination to what will happen and as less indifference in reasoning is best, it follows that in conceiving freedom as a perfection, and as it is in God and in the blessed intellects insofar as they are perfect, it must be opposed to *bondage*, and consequently it must be said that we are free insofar as we are determined to follow the perfection of our nature, which is to say, reason; but that we are slaves insofar as we follow passions and customs or the unthinking impulses that reason has not beforehand formed into a habit of doing well. It is also insofar as we follow this perfection of our nature that we are said *to act*, and to make the rule for other things in the harmony of the universe; and insofar as we are imperfect, we are said *to suffer*, and to be subject to external things, although in a certain metaphysical sense, which I have explained in my system of the union of the soul and the body, there is spontaneity in everything which happens to us. Everything that concerns us can be considered as derived from our own nature.

But it will be said that, if everything is certain and determined, it is completely useless that I try to do good; for although I do try, what must happen will happen. This is the sophism that the ancients previously called *lazy reason* (logon argon), which occurs whether one speaks in a Christian way and about salvation, or one speaks about matters of life and in a philosophical way. But the response is at hand: if it is determined that so-and-so will be ruined, then without a doubt that will happen, not in spite of what he does, but because he will be the author of his own fortune, and if he neglects himself, he will ruin himself. If you break your neck on the steps, you will do what is necessary for that, because you could not be determined to an effect without being predetermined to the causes. And God's understanding or foreknowledge corresponds to the nature of things.

Consequently, when you yourself are damned, so to speak, in the truth of events, you yourself are also damned in the idea that God has of them.

I find that people come up with false ideas in philosophy, and even difficulties unnecessary in theology, by detaching one decree of God from another. It can be imagined, according to some, that God resolves to save so-and-so, for example, completely apart from the sequence of things, and that afterwards God thinks about what is needed in order to save him. And according to others, it can be imagined that God begins the election by foreknowledge or predetermination of faith. People certainly recognize that there is no temporal priority in these decrees of God, but they always want to find a priority of nature in them, which they call *in signo rationis* [in the sign of reason]. And very great controversies are built thereon. But we should consider that God, while acting with perfect wisdom, does not form any decree without keeping in mind all the causes and all the effects in the whole universe, because of the connection of all things. Therefore it would be best to say that God only forms a single decree, which is the one to choose this universe from among the other possible universes, and in this decree everything is included, without there being need to look for order among the particular decrees, as if one were independent of the others.

Moreover, Sir, we imagine ourselves having a power to believe and to will what we like, but there is no basis for this power: we do not will to will, but to do and have; we do not choose our wills, because this would be on the basis of other will, and so on to infinity, but we choose the objects; this choice or this will has its causes, but as we are ignorant of them and as they are quite often hidden, we believe ourselves to be independent of them, just as we walk and jump without thinking about the circulation of blood necessary for this. And it is this chimera of an imaginary independence which pitches us against the consideration of determination, and which leads us to believe that there are difficulties there when in fact there are not. Also, when one wants to express these difficulties in a clear and precise manner and with order, they disappear, demonstrating that they have no foundation. And I have often challenged intelligent people to provide these difficulties and to put them forward in a clear and precise manner, and above all in writing. Nevertheless it is true that we have spontaneity within ourselves, and that we are the masters of our actions, which is to say that we choose what we will; but we will what we find good, which depends on our taste and the objects, and not on our choice. And when by a whim, or perhaps in order to demonstrate our freedom, we choose what we could not otherwise think is good, it is because the pleasure of acting against the ordinary forms a part of the object, and our spirit of contrariness forms a part of our taste. But ultimately it always remains true that there is contingency in our actions, and that basically our predetermination is only an inclination, and not a necessity. Within this lies a wonderful secret of nature, which forms the basis of contingency, which the Scholastics used to look for when considering *de radice contingentiae* [the origin of contingency], and which I hope to clearly explain one day.

With regard to the law of reward and punishment, which it is customary to put forward as contrary to the certitude or determination of events and the future contingent actions of men, on the pretext that he who is not free does not deserve to be punished or praised, it is easy to demonstrate that there is no difficulty whatsoever. For it always remains true that the hope of reward contributes to making one do good, and the fear of punishment makes one refrain from doing evil, which is also the whole point of them. Thus these promises and threats form part of the causes of the effect, and are predetermined just as much as the effect. It is therefore sufficient that actions are voluntary, without needing to be indifferent. And it is even possible to say that if men were indifferent, and were not inclined to act on the basis of causes, they would not be concerned about punishments or rewards, and would not be led to the good by these means, which as a consequence would become useless. Moreover, it is sometimes necessary to remove the rotten members, who are bad even when their evil does not depend on themselves, as when a mangy sheep is removed from the flock, and when a mad person is locked up. Not to mention that there is an order of justice which also demands some satisfaction beyond the amendment and the example. But without entering into that, it is sufficient to have demonstrated that the usefulness of punishments and rewards, of threats and promises, does indeed exist, in order to say that their law also exists, because the law is grounded in the general usefulness.

Thus this response is ultimately the same as the one we gave above to *lazy reason*, which is that events, although certain and foreseen, do not happen in spite of what one does, but that in doing what is fitting one makes them happen. And this is the case with regard to punishments and rewards, just as with regard to other means which one makes use of in order to produce some effect.

You have made a very good distinction, Sir, together with the theologians, between the known and the unknown will of God, or rather between the wills of God on law, which make use of rules, and his wills on facts. Those two kinds of will are different without being contraries, and it can even be said that the wills concerning facts are subordinated to the first ones. But we can only regulate ourselves on the known will of God, which is general, which is to say on the orders that he has given us; and in doing it or not doing it, we ourselves contribute to making a success of his unknown will concerning facts, which is particular, or rather individual, upon which one cannot regulate oneself. Such are his wills concerning election, stubbornness, term of penitence, and other similar things, about which there is never complete certainty before the event, and about which we ought not to dispute or come up with conclusions without foundation, conclusions capable of distressing some and causing them to despair, and of producing libertines and giving security to others. We cannot determine what will happen to so-and-so in particular, and what grace God will grant to him; but we can be assured in general that the necessary grace will never be lacking for the one who has good will, and that the wicked man who comes back to a true repentance is never rejected, but that it is very difficult to come to it when one has scorned it for a long time; that Jesus Christ is the principle of salvation and election, and other similar rules, founded in the universal and known will of God.

You have also remarked aptly, Sir, about that passage in the *Acts of the Apostles* in which St. Paul has a vision which assures him that God has given him the lives of all those who sail with him, without any of them needing to perish in shipwreck.[7] Nevertheless the same St. Paul does not fail to say to the centurion: if those seamen save themselves with the lifeboat, as is their intention, we will not be able to be saved;[8] note that the preservation, completely predetermined as it was, came with its necessary causes and conditions. Thus God, having granted this preservation to St. Paul, also granted him the insight to see what was necessary, and the authority to prevent the disorder that was contrary to it.

There is also the difficulty of prayers and wishes, and it is often said, when one thinks of how everything is arranged in advance, that vows and wishes serve no purpose. But there is nothing without effect in the whole of nature, and vows show our good will, which is never without reward, although it is not always exactly and precisely such as we would wish it; what is more, by dint of wishing, we often apply ourselves to the object, and by dint of prayer, we find the insights which help us to succeed, not to mention those extraordinary cases, such as when someone stopped in a place of prayer failed to be found by his enemies who waited for him. But even in the things that are outside our reach, prayers are useful, because the idea or the foreknowledge of our prayers aided the divine understanding when it arranged the universe, and this foreknowledge has thus formed a part of the causes or motives in the will of God, just as the foreknowledge or expectation of punishments and rewards, according to what we have demonstrated, is one of the motives of the will of men; because God has regard for everything, but especially for good people and their good will, whom he favours as much as the harmony of the universe will permit, all the more since the order of bodies is made to serve the order of minds. Thus the connection of things allows one to say that the prayers of good people divert public or private disasters and attract good fortune (although this is not always in a recognizable manner) by a physical influence or even by a present and new moral influence, just as if God allows himself to be diverted from what he has resolved to do; because it is at the very beginning of things, and especially when he made a resolution, that they have already exercised their effect.

Some, not being able to deny these principles or to produce another tenable system, remonstrate against the consequences for lack of good understanding: they say that in this way nothing would be praiseworthy or blameworthy, and that God would be unjust, cruel, and the author of evil. But we have already demonstrated the usefulness of laws, punishments, rewards and prayers and their fittingness in our system. The same applies to blame and praise, which are actually a kind of punishment or reward. And granting that God has chosen the best, as his perfection requires of him, it must be the case that permitting sin is better than excluding it, since it happens. But if someone wants to use this doubt to overturn the divine perfections, and destroy God himself by denying his power or at least his foreknowledge with a few Socinians or Demisocinians, it is easy to show him that there is no need to go to these extremes, which are moreover completely absurd, because God found sin and other evils that occur contained in the idea of this possible universe, which he has judged the best, and which he wills above all others because of the good in it. Thus it cannot be said that he wills evil and misery, but only that he permits it, and neither could be excluded from it without choosing another universe which, by the same supposition that we just made, would not be the best, as the best is the one that God has in fact chosen, all allowances being made. It cannot be said that God does evil, because the good, the perfection, the positive reality, is from him alone; boundaries or limits, which are something of the negative because they deny further perfection, are distinctive of creatures since they are finite, and they alone bring about ignorance, malice and evil.[9]

B. Contingency and Necessity[10]

1. Middle knowledge (November 1677)[11]

That greatest principle, *nothing is without a reason*, ends most disputes in metaphysics. For that, it seems, cannot be denied by the Scholastics – nothing happens without God being able to give a reason, if he wishes, why it should have happened rather than not. Moreover, the same can be said with regard to future conditionals, about which Fonseca and Molina have introduced the concept of middle knowledge.[12] God knows what the future would have been for an infant if it had grown up, but also he could give the reason for his own knowledge of this if he wished to do so, to overcome anyone who doubted him, whereas any man might also be able to do it but only in an imperfect way. Therefore God's knowledge does not consist in some vision, which is imperfect and *a posteriori*, but in his *a priori* knowledge of the cause. Let us suppose that Peter is placed in some specified circumstances, with some specified assistance of grace; and God permits me to ask him what Peter is going to do in this situation. I do not doubt that God would be able to respond with something certain and infallible, though I am amazed that some Scholastics have dared to have doubts with regard to this matter. Now let us assume that God answers that Peter is going to reject grace. I then ask whether God is able to give a reason for his own pronouncement, so that he can also make me aware of the outcome. If we say that God cannot give it then his knowledge of it will be imperfect, and if we say that he can give it then evidently the concept of middle knowledge will be overthrown. According to true philosophers and St. Augustine,[13] the reason why God knows the actions of things, necessary or free, absolute or conditional, is his perfect knowledge of the nature of these actions, just as the geometer knows what can be proved with a compass and a ruler in any proposition; or what will be the effect of a given machine, if it is fitted with given appliances and powers. Let us assume that Paul is placed in the same circumstances in which Peter is also placed and with the same assistance, and that God says to me that Peter is then going to reject grace, while Paul is going to accept it; it is certainly necessary that there is some reason for this difference, but it cannot be found anywhere other than from 'Peterness' and 'Paulness', i.e. from the nature of Paul's will and the nature of Peter's will, and this difference in their two freedoms brings it about that one chooses this and the other that. But it is also necessary that this difference in the succession of thoughts towards this choice is known to God, and if he deigned to explain it to me I would understand, and so I would obtain full knowledge of a future conditional event *a priori*. According to the inventors of *middle knowledge*, God would not be able to give a reason for his pronouncement, nor explain it to me. This is the only thing he could say to anyone who asked why he pronounced the future to be thus: that he sees this action represented in this way in that great mirror set within himself, in which all things, present, future, absolute or conditional, are displayed. This knowledge is purely empirical, and would not satisfy God because he would not understand the reason why this rather than that is represented in the mirror, just like a person who discovers numbers calculated in tables though he himself is unable to calculate them. God knows the future absolutely because he knows what he has decreed, and he knows future conditionals because he knows what he is going to decree. And he knows what he is going to decree because he knows what will be best in that particular case, for he is going to decree the best. If not, it will follow that God cannot know for certain what he himself will do in this particular case. Scotus' famous view, that the divine intellect knows nothing (of matters of fact) that it has not determined, would otherwise become worthless.[14] The opinion of Vasquez, that the will cannot choose from two objects unless the goodness of one of them is represented more strongly, is excellent.[15]

2. On freedom from necessity in choosing (summer 1680–summer 1684)[16]

It seems it can be said: it is certain and infallible that the mind determines itself towards the greatest apparent good. There has never been given a contrary example where error, or even thoughtlessness, did not precede a sin, as it appears in the sin of the first man, who believed that he would be like God through the use of the fruit.

Meanwhile it also needs to be said that although it may be certain, nevertheless *it is not necessary but free*, because the mind is determined not by external things but by itself.

For St. Thomas has excellently located freedom in the power of self-determination or of acting upon oneself.[17] From which it is also evident how God knows beforehand which free acts are about to happen, because he knows in advance what will appear to a mind as the greatest good.

Therefore from various possible free creatures God has chosen the one which will determine itself by reasons of good, because this was in keeping with the first free decree of God, with regard to the most perfect being chosen.

It is to be understood that the nature of the mind is such that it would do something even if all beings outside itself (besides God) were at rest, because it would contemplate God and itself and the ideas of possible things. This cannot be said about the body, for that must be pushed by something in order to be set in motion. And in this power, to determine itself to action, consists the nature of freedom.

God foresaw that Adam was going to sin if he fell into the temptation of the fruit, so why has he not changed the series of things? I answer: because God knew this series of things was going to be more perfect than any other, therefore he did not change it. But, you will say, *did he therefore will that Adam should sin*? I answer by denying the consequence. But he willed that series from which he knew it followed that Adam was going to sin. I deny this, for it did not follow that Adam was going to sin, because he sinned freely. Yet it is true that he willed that series in which it was certain that Adam was going to sin. This cannot be denied. Therefore he willed Adam to sin? That does not follow, for he only permitted it. No one, however, who accepts the omniscience of God can deny that he certainly knew that Adam was going to sin, if he was created by him, or that he would fall when presented with the temptation of the fruit. God does not want sin, i.e. he wants to prevent it, insofar as it can be done through the harmony of things. Paul's depth of riches[18] is the harmony of things which exceeds the capacity of the human mind, although our mind knows that it exists.

It is best to say that freedom exists in minds not so much by compulsion but by necessity, and although it is certain and inevitable that God always chooses the most perfect, whether in fact the best, or most expedient to his own glory, and men always choose the apparent best, nevertheless it is not for that reason necessary, otherwise it would follow that nothing is possible except that which is actually created, whereas there are infinite possibles (namely whatever does not imply contradiction) which are not chosen by God. Hence it is evident that God freely chooses the most perfect. The first of God's free decrees is that he wills always to act in accordance with his own glory, i.e. in the most perfect way. From this come all other decrees. Therefore since God is free from necessity with regard to choosing the actual best good, even man, created of course in God's image, will be free from necessity with regard to choosing the apparent good, although it is always certain that he will choose what seems the best. But these things do not obstruct certainty.

Now the opinion of Hobbes and Wyclif,[19] who say that nothing is possible except what actually happens, i.e. that everything is necessary, must be resisted. If they had said that everything is certain and infallible, they would have said it right, for there are infinite possibilities which do not happen.

The root of human freedom lies in God's image. Although God always chooses the best (and if another omniscient being were imagined, he would be able to say beforehand what God would choose) nevertheless he chooses freely, because what he does not choose remains possible by its own nature, and so its opposite is not necessary. Man is free in the same way, so that although from two options he always chooses the one that appears best, nevertheless he does not choose through necessity. For it is one thing always to be able to give a reason why he chooses, but quite another thing to say that the choice is necessary; reasons incline, they do not necessitate, although what they incline towards follows as certain. But since in beasts there is no reflection or action upon themselves, so there is no free decree with regard to their own actions. It can be said that all things have a certain hypothetical necessity, not of essence but of existence, i.e. of secondary action; or the necessity of things originates not from their essence but from the will of God, since from the assumed decree of God all things are necessary.

Everything is possible for God except what includes imperfection.

Imperfection includes sin, for instance to damn someone innocent.

The damnation of an innocent man is indeed possible in itself, i.e. it does not imply a contradiction, but it is not possible for God. More correctly, the eternal damnation of an innocent man seems to be from that number of things of which the essence does not in fact imply a contradiction because it can be completely understood, but nevertheless its existing implies a contradiction. For we do not need to examine the whole harmony of things in order to know whether God is going to eternally damn someone innocent.

That from the more perfect God could choose the less perfect does not imply an imperfection in God, nor is it contrary to his power but to his will, or his first decree. And it does not imply a contradiction for him to decide otherwise.

God has decided by his creation to procure his own glory, so that his wisdom would also be recognized by others, i.e. he decided to create creatures according to his own likeness, and to establish all things in such a way that they are the most perfect with respect to rational creatures. That is, so that everything will be more pleasing to them the more they penetrate into the interior of things. This is the first of God's decrees, and on this basis everything else follows by necessary consequence. This decree of God concerning the creation of things is not a proposition whose contrary implies a contradiction, i.e. it is not necessary for other things besides God to exist, but it is free.

The reason why God chooses the most perfect cannot be given, other than because he wills it, i.e. because it is the first divine will to choose the most perfect. That is, this follows not from things themselves, but purely from the fact that God wills. And certainly he wills freely, because outside of his will no reason can be given for why he wills. For I define 'free' as that for which no reason can be given other than the will; therefore nothing exists without a reason, but that reason is intrinsic to the will. And in this there consists the true nature of the spontaneous, that it is a principle, but not an external one. And so there is some freedom in every mind, and God concurs with the action of a mind, but not so as to constitute the first act of the mind, otherwise no mind would act, but only God himself.

Our mind is indifferent with regard to reasons, i.e. there is no reason so strong in this life which sufficiently penetrates the mind so that it is not easily able to be diverted from considering it, and with that distraction it will always be able to doubt, because it does not remember the demonstration perfectly. But once the beatific vision is obtained, the mind cannot be wrested from it, or have doubts about the things which it sees.

Can this proposition, that 'God chooses the most perfect', be demonstrated from the nature of God? I say that it can be demonstrated once his will is known. But can it be demonstrated that he has such a will? I say that it is not demonstrable *a priori*, but that it is a first proposition, i.e. it is identical.

Whoever considers right, will admit this to me: just as the principle of contradiction is the origin of everything that can be known about essences, so there must be some first principle about existences, supposing that not all possibles exist.

The first principle about existences is this proposition: *God wills to choose the most perfect*. This proposition cannot be demonstrated; it is the first of all propositions of fact, i.e. the origin of all contingent existence. It is entirely the same thing to say that *God is free*, and to say that *this proposition is an indemonstrable principle*. For if a reason can be given for this first divine decree, by that very fact God would not have decided it freely. Therefore I say this proposition can be compared to identities. For just as *A is A* or *a thing is equal to itself* cannot be demonstrated, so also *God wills the most perfect*. This proposition is the origin of the transition from possibility to existence of creatures. But you will ask whether the contrary implies a contradiction, namely that God does not choose the most perfect. I say that it does not imply a contradiction, unless the will of God is already assumed. For God wills to will to choose the most perfect, and wills the will to will, and so on to infinity, because such infinite reflections happen to God, however they do not happen to a creature. The whole mystery therefore consists in this, that God has not only decided to do the most perfect, but has also decided to decide. And hence no sign can be imagined which is not preceded naturally by another sign in respect of which a decision has already been made. For generally it is to be held that there is no decree that God has not decreed by another decree prior in nature, in accordance with the nature of perfect freedom, outside of which there is no reason. And this answers perfectly everyone who weakens divine freedom, and in place of Vasquez's circle we have a progression to infinity (for Vasquez believed that God wills a thing because it is going to exist, and the thing is going to exist because God wills it). For if anyone will ask from me the reason *why God decided to create Adam*, I say: *because he decided to make the most perfect*. If you now ask me *why he decided to make the most perfect, or why he wills the most perfect* (for what is 'to will' other than 'to decide to do'?) I answer that *he willed it freely*, i.e. *because he willed it*. And he willed it because he willed to will, and so on to infinity. Hence it is evident that the will of God excludes anything prior to itself, and it cannot be demonstrated that this will is the divine will to decide with regard to the most perfect, unless another will is assumed. But because a creature is not able to choose[20] infinite acts at the same time, its freedom therefore consists in the power to divert the mind towards other thoughts. But why does it divert the mind? On account of some trouble in the thought itself, and the pleasure in other thoughts. Is the mind therefore determined by trouble and pleasure? Certainly not. Although it always inclines towards the direction where the immediate greater good is apparent, nevertheless it inclines freely so that it is able to choose another path, because it acts spontaneously.

3. A note on freedom and necessity (1680–1684?)[21]

The necessity of the consequence is when something follows from another thing by a necessary consequence. Absolute necessity is when the contrary of a thing implies contradiction. From the essence of God or from supreme perfection it follows, certainly and so to speak by a necessary consequence, that God chooses the best, yet he chooses the best freely, because in the best itself there is no absolute necessity, otherwise its contrary would imply a contradiction and only the best would be possible, but then everything else would be impossible, contrary to the hypothesis. And so with a circle or triangle each claiming existence, God freely chooses the circle (so we may imagine), although he chooses it because of its greater beauty. But on the other hand he does not choose between a circle of uniform and non-uniform circumference, but on the assumption that a circle is to be created he will necessarily create it uniform, and it can be said absolutely that God cannot choose a deformed circle because it is impossible by its own nature, and so it is absolutely necessary that it be rejected.

The root of freedom in God is the possibility or contingency of things, by which it happens that innumerable things are found which are neither necessary nor impossible, from which God chooses those which do most to testify to his own glory. The root of freedom in man is the divine image, because God certainly willed to create man free and he has made it so that man would be moved only by some consideration of his own good, just as God only has reason for choosing his own glory, but the distinction is this: that while man can be mistaken because of a defect in the original creature, God cannot.

4. On contingency (spring–autumn 1689?)[22]

In God, existence does not differ from essence, or what is the same thing, it is essential for God to exist. Hence God is a necessary being.

Creatures are contingent, that is, their existence does not follow from their essence.

Necessary truths are those that can be demonstrated through an analysis of terms, so that in the end they pass into identities, just as in algebra the substitution of values in the end produces an identical equation. That is, necessary truths depend on the principle of contradiction.

Contingent truths cannot be reduced to the principle of contradiction, otherwise everything would be necessary and nothing would be possible other than what actually attains existence.

Nevertheless, because we say that both God and creatures exist and we say that necessary propositions are true no less than contingent ones, it is necessary that there be some concept common to contingent existence and essential truth.

In my opinion it is common to every truth that a reason can be given for a (non-identical) proposition; in necessary propositions, it necessitates; in contingent propositions, it inclines. And this seems to be common to existing things, both necessary and contingent, that they have more reason for existing than others which might be assumed in their place.

Every true universal affirmative proposition, whether necessary or contingent, has this, so that there is some connection between the predicate and the subject. And indeed in those propositions which are identical, the connection is self-evident. In the others it must appear through the analysis of terms.

And here is revealed the secret distinction between necessary and contingent truths, which will not easily be understood except by those who have some knowledge of mathematics, namely that in necessary propositions, when the analysis is continued for a time, we arrive at an identical equation; and this is how to demonstrate a truth in geometrical rigour. In contingent propositions, however, the analysis continues to infinity through reasons of reasons, so that we never have a full demonstration, although there is always an underlying reason for the truth, even if it is only perfectly understood by God, who alone penetrates an infinite series in one stroke of the mind.

The matter can be illustrated with an appropriate example from geometry and numbers. Just as in necessary propositions, where, through a continual analysis of the predicate and the subject, a thing can at last be brought to the point where it is apparent that the concept of the predicate is in the subject, so it is in the case of numbers, where, through a continual analysis (of successive divisions) we can finally arrive at a common measure. But just as in incommensurables there is also a proportion or comparison, even though the resolution proceeds to infinity and never comes to an end, as has been demonstrated by Euclid, so also in contingent truths there is a connection of the terms, i.e. there is truth, even if it cannot be reduced to the principle of contradiction or necessity through an analysis into identities.

It can be asked whether this proposition: *God chooses the best* is necessary, or whether it is one of, and even the first of, his free decrees.

Likewise, it can be asked, in a similar vein, whether this proposition is necessary: *nothing exists without there being a greater reason for existing than for not existing*.

It is certain that in every truth there is a connection between subject and predicate. Therefore, when it is said that *a sinning Adam exists*, it is necessary that there is something in this possible concept a *sinning Adam* on account of which it may be said to exist.

It seems that we must concede that God only ever acts wisely, i.e. so that he who knew his reasons would recognize and worship his supreme justice, goodness, and wisdom. Consequently there never seems to be a case of God acting out of pure pleasure, which is not at the same time pleasing for the right reason.

Because we cannot know the true formal reason for existence in any particular case, since it involves a progression to infinity, it is therefore sufficient for us to know a contingent truth *a posteriori*, namely through experience; and yet, at the same time, to hold, universally and generally, that principle inserted into our mind by God, which is confirmed both by reason and experience (insofar as we are able to penetrate into things), that nothing happens without a reason, and that from a pair of opposites the one which has more reason always happens.

And just as God himself has decreed to act always and only according to the true reasons of wisdom, so he has created rational creatures in such a way that they only act according to prevailing or inclining reasons, whether true or apparent.

Unless there were such a principle, a substitute for reason, there would be no principle of truth in contingent things, because the principle of contradiction is certainly not itself contingent.

We must hold for certain that not all possibles attain existence, otherwise no story could be imagined that did not exist somewhere or at some time. Indeed, it does not seem possible that all possibles should exist, because they mutually impede each other. And there are an infinite series of possibles, but one series certainly cannot be inside another, since each one is entire in itself.

From these two propositions, everything else follows:

1) God always acts with the mark of perfection or wisdom.
2) Not every possible attains existence.

To which can be added:

3) In every true universal affirmative proposition the predicate is in the subject, i.e., there is a connection between predicate and subject.

Assuming that this proposition: *the proposition that has the greater reason for existing exists* is necessary, we must see whether it follows that the proposition that has the greater reason for existing is necessary. But this consequence is rightly denied. For if the definition of a necessary proposition is that its truth can be demonstrated with geometrical rigour, then it can indeed be the case that this proposition can be demonstrated: *every truth and only a truth has a greater reason,* or this: *God always acts most wisely.* But it will not therefore be possible to demonstrate this proposition: *contingent proposition A has a greater reason or contingent proposition A conforms to divine wisdom.* And therefore it does not actually follow that contingent proposition A is necessary. And therefore, although it should be conceded that it is necessary that God choose the best, or that the best is necessary, nevertheless it does not follow that what is chosen is necessary, because there is no demonstration that it is the best. And here the distinction between the necessity of the consequence and the necessity of the consequent in some way holds good, so that in the end the best is necessary by the necessity of the consequence, not of the consequent. This is because, by the very fact that it is supposed to be the best, from the hypothesis which we have agreed, it is necessary because of God's infallible choice of the best.

It seems safer to attribute to God the most perfect manner of operation. In creatures it is not exactly certain that they will act according to the greatest apparent reason, since this proposition cannot be demonstrated in their case.

5. Notes on Pierre Bayle's *Reply to the Questions from a Provincial* (1706)[23]

God necessarily wills the work most worthy of his wisdom.[24] I answer: God wills it freely, because what we call free is when the contrary does not imply contradiction. But it implies that God does not choose the best.[25] I do not know whether one could say that this is absolutely implied. However, if that was the case, this is how we are able to proceed: 'that which is best is chosen' – this proposition is necessary, very well. 'This is the best' – this proposition is true, but it is not demonstrable by a demonstration that shows that the contrary implies contradiction. It is a contingent truth. 'Therefore this is chosen.' The conclusion follows the weaker part. Therefore this conclusion is not necessary either.

Now, I do not recognize any proposition as necessary which cannot be demonstrated by a reduction to one whose contrary implies contradiction. It is the same argument: 'God necessarily wills the work most worthy of his wisdom.' I say that he wills it, but not necessarily, because although this work is the most worthy, that is not a necessary truth. It is true that this proposition, 'God wills the work most worthy of him', is necessary. But it is not true that he wills it necessarily. For this proposition, 'this work is the most worthy', is not a necessary truth, it is an indemonstrable, contingent truth of fact. I believe that it can generally be said that this proposition is necessary: 'his will will act following the greatest inclination'. But it does not follow that it will act necessarily. In the same way it is necessary that future contingents are determined, but it is not true that they are determined necessarily, that is to say, that they are not contingent. The necessary proposition 'A is B.' Is this not then true: 'A is necessarily B'? This is a necessary proposition: 'God wills the better.' So is it therefore the case that 'God necessarily wills the better'? I answer that 'necessarily' can be applied to the copula, but not to what is contained in the copula. God is necessarily he who wills the best. But not he who necessarily wills the best. Because he wills freely. In the same way it is permitted to say: 'A man wills to walk.' This proposition is contingent by necessity, but it does not therefore become a necessary contingent.

It is necessary that God wills the best, but by a will that is not necessary, i.e. by his free will. That is, it is necessary that God wills the best, but not by necessity. It is necessary that a contingent is of determined truth, but by a determination that is not necessary. It is necessary that the soul chooses that towards which the reason of choice inclines it, although by a choice which is not necessary. It is better to say: God, who because of his freedom can clearly create nothing, can also create the lesser; but the reason which brings it about that he creates something, also brings it about that he produces the best in accordance with what the measure of things has decreed – a reason, I say, which inclines but does not necessitate. But he is not able to do or will moral evil.

Notes

1 A VI iv 1406–9. French.

2 G VII 109–11. French.

3 Gr 478–86. French.

4 Here Leibniz originally wrote: 'When it is impossible that something should not exist, we say that it is necessary.'

5 Thomas Hobbes, *On Body*, part II, chapter 10 arts. 4–5; Spinoza, *Ethics*, book 1, proposition 16; Descartes, *Principles of Philosophy*, part 3, article 47.

6 See Cicero, *The Nature of the Gods* 1, 69.

7 Acts 27:24.

8 Acts 27:31.

9 Here Leibniz originally wrote: 'There are opponents of a different kind, and who throw themselves into the other extreme: these are the disciples of Hobbes and Spinoza, who, not being at all concerned whether there is a God, or at least whether he is good or not, claim that everything happens by a fatal necessity, absolute or without choice, and that God is the author of evil, even moral evil, and wills it just as he wills good, and even that perfection and true good is only in our mind, and is chimerical in the nature of things; that also everything possible, good and bad, happens equally in its own time, as if God, according to Spinoza, has the power but not the understanding or will that would render him capable of choice. But we have already laid the foundations which destroy an error so pernicious, which result from what these authors did not yet know in their times of the wonderful beauty and the infinite divine artifice in the universe, which does not allow atoms or void or even purely material substance; which does not want the necessity which is absolute but absurd, and chance; which works as if governed by two rules, which correspond to each other exactly, one of final causes, the other of

efficient causes; which subjugates the material world, or the world of bodies, to that of minds, and the physical to the moral, mechanism to metaphysical reality, abstract notions to complete notions, phenomena or results to true substances, which are only unities and always subsist; which demands a perfect connection of all things and a complete order, such that it is impossible that anything better and greater be conceived. And this is what is apparent, more than ever, through the new system of pre-established harmony, explained elsewhere, which gives a completely different face to the union, as different in respect of its superiority over the one which was previously given, as the system of Copernicus is over the one ordinarily given to the visible world.'

10 See also III.A.3.

11 A VI iv 1373–4. Latin.

12 Peter Fonseca, *Commentaria in libros Metaphysicorum Aristotelis* (1604), vol. 3 book 6, ch.2, q.4, secs 8–10; Luis de Molina, *Concordia* (1588), q.14, art. 13, disp. 50.

13 St. Augustine, *City of God*, book 11, chapter 21.

14 John Duns Scotus, *Quaestiones in lib. I sententiarium*, dist. 39, q.5, n.23.

15 Gabriel Vasquez, *Commentariorum ac disputationum in primam secundae S. Thomae. Tomus primus* (1599).

16 A VI iv 1450–5. Latin.

17 Aquinas, *Summa Theologicae*, 1q83a1–3.

18 Romans 11.33.

19 For Hobbes, see note 5 above. John Wyclif, *Dialogorum libri quattuor* (1525), book 3, chapter 8.

20 Reading *eligere* for *elicere*.

21 A VI iv 2577. Latin. From Leibniz's notes on Cardinal Bellarmine's *Disputationes de controversiis christianae fidei* (1617–20).

22 A VI iv 1649–52. Latin.

23 Gr 493–4. French and Latin.

24 A claim made in chapter 151 of Bayle's *Réponse aux Questions d'un Provincial* (1706). What follows is Leibniz's response to it.

25 Here Leibniz originally wrote: 'This is what I do not dare to say absolutely, but he will choose it.'

IV. SCIENCE

A. Matter and Body[1]

1. A demonstration against atoms taken from the contact of atoms (23–24 October 1690)[2]

23 October 1690.

DEFINITION I. A thing is distinguished from other things in two ways, either through itself or extrinsically. A thing is distinguished from another through itself when the way of distinguishing it is by a consideration of the thing alone, with no operation on the thing and no change brought about in the thing. Extrinsically, when something new in the thing is revealed by an external consideration of it, which is not discovered in something else. Thus a sphere and a cube can be distinguished not only by observing them, but also by operation: by observation, because no angles are found in the former, of which there are eight in a cube; by operation, in that if both are placed on a flat incline, the sphere will descend by rolling, while the cube remains level (while slipping).

AXIOM. Whatever is distinguishable extrinsically from something else is also distinguishable through itself.[3]

For example there may be two coins from the same press, one made out of true gold, the other made out of fake gold, which are easily distinguished extrinsically by a blow of a hammer. I certainly say that before the blow the distinctions in the actual composition of each could be discovered by careful consideration with the naked or assisted eye. And although our visual acuity may not be able to penetrate so far, there are nevertheless distinctions within and they could be discovered by a more observant creature (for instance by an angel).

OBSERVATION. Certain bodies are broken up by each other.

ACCEPTED HYPOTHESIS. Matter is uniform, that is, with motion and shape removed, it is everywhere alike.

DEFINITION II. An atom is a body that cannot be broken up.

POSTULATE: If atoms exist, we may assume them to be of any shape and size whatever.

THEOREM

It cannot be the case that all bodies are composed of atoms.

Let us assume (by the postulate) three atoms *A*, *B* and *C*, of which *A* is cubical but *B* and *C* are triangular prisms which compose cube *D*, which is similar and equal to the aforementioned *A*. Cube *D* cannot be distinguished through itself from cube *A* (by the accepted hypothesis). Therefore they will not be able to be distinguished extrinsically (by axiom 1). Therefore if other bodies crash into cube *D*, atoms *B* and *C* will either be separable or not. If they are separable then the same bodies crashing into cube *A* in the same way will be able to break it up into parts, otherwise *A* and *B*[4] could be distinguished extrinsically (by definition 1), the contrary of which has been shown. But if cube *A* is broken up into parts, it will not be an atom (by definition 2), as was supposed. But if other bodies are unable to break up cube *D* into its component parts again, it follows that through contact an atom is made out of non-atoms. And the same will be true no matter what shape of atom is considered. Hence it follows that atoms which have struck each other once cannot be broken up again. Now if all bodies are composed from atoms then bodies only touch each other through their atoms. And therefore they cannot be broken up after contact, unless an atom of one body may be broken away from an atom of another, which we have shown[5] cannot happen. But bodies [can?]

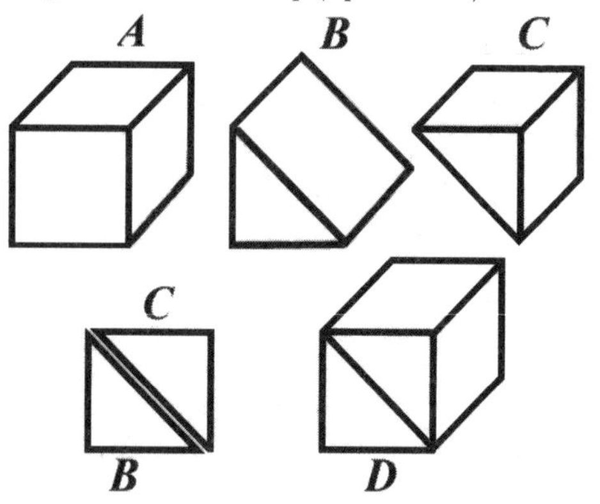

not be broken up . . . [6] And so it is not true that all bodies are composed from atoms. Q.E.D.

Scholion to the demonstration against atoms taken from the contact of atoms

24 October 1690.

I do not see what response can be made to the demonstration unless the postulate is denied. For we have demanded that this postulate is conceded to us: if atoms exist, it is possible that they assume any shape or size whatever. It seems that if nothing else we have grounds to say that there can be no atoms whose parts are only joined by a point or a line. And so (for example) there cannot be an atom such as one composed from two spheres touching each other. But if spherical atoms exist, or atoms bounded by other kinds of curved surfaces, they will never touch each other except at a point, and so they will never compose a body like an atom. I believe this can be pursued further, firstly if the contact on the surface is the cause of stability, it will follow that there will be a greater stability when the surface is greater. Hence atoms would not be equally stable. And so a certain force needed to break them up could be determined, by which the stabilities could be measured. I do not see where we could discover such a force, if it is not in the motion of bodies, unless we invoke some kinds of spiritual forces, but it is impossible to understand how they act on bodies. But if the stability of all atoms is equal, and it does not matter how much contact there is, then contact along a line, or even at a point, will be sufficient.

Another consequence is this: we have at least demonstrated that bodies cannot be composed from atoms bounded by plane faces. But apart from the fact that it can be doubted whether true curved lines actually exist, this exception does not seem to be in accordance with the reasons of things, so that if a composition from atoms is possible it must necessarily happen through bodies without a plane surface.

The third consequence is this: not only atoms of flat surfaces but also those of concave surfaces must be removed from nature. Otherwise it will be possible to make atoms from the non-atom whenever it happens that the concave surface of one atom is connected to the convex surface of another, and this will keep happening until it comes to pass that all atoms with concave surfaces are filled by as many convex surfaces existing in nature. But this restriction likewise does not seem to be in accordance with the reasons of things. And in general, if anyone, in order to escape the force of our demonstration, denies that any atoms exist other than perfectly spherical atoms, then he contrives something that suits later arguments, but it does not correspond to the principal reasons and greatness of nature. To put it briefly: from the hypothesis of atoms I am able to deduce absurd consequences, provided that I am allowed to assign the size, shape and motion to atoms that I wish.[7]

Appendix to the demonstration against atoms, taken from the contact of atoms

If anyone denies that there could be atoms whose parts touch each other only at a point or along a line, and that this is all the surface contact that is needed for cohesion, so that he avoids the power of our demonstration, he will impale himself upon other new difficulties.

For if the cohesion arises from surface contact, we can imagine a case in which one atom is unable to touch another atom; for when a part of the face of atom *B* is congruent with a part of the face of atom $_3A$, not only will they not be able to be broken apart and torn away, but also one will not be able to slide over the other, for they touch each other on the surface. Indeed, what is more amazing, atom *A* coming from position $_1A$ by its own motion to position $_2A$ is then so situated that it cannot proceed further because it will touch atom *B*, whereupon it will be stopped without any obstacle, as if a spell had been cast on it. Nor is it sufficient to say that no such atoms exist, or that no others exist in nature except the spherical or at least those bounded by convex surfaces. For if atoms bounded by convex faces are possible, that is sufficient to establish that atoms bounded by plane or concave faces are possible, and from their supposed possibility arises an absurd situation, from which it follows that convex atoms are not admissible either.

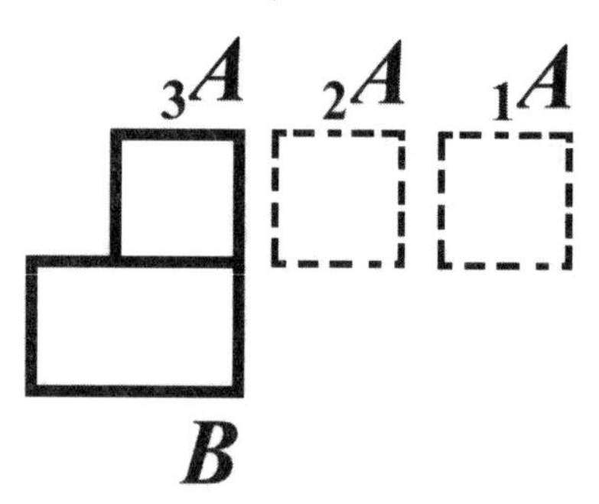

But if anyone, realizing this, were now to require for cohesion not only greater surface contact but also that the atoms touching each other should be at rest, in order for one atom to be prevented from sliding on top of another, he would be unable to provide a proof of his own argument, nor is it apparent why the nature and force of the present state, which is contact, should depend on the previous state, namely that the present contact should produce cohesion if it has remained for some time in the same place, as if some accustoming is necessary, from which it would also follow that stability is increased by time, and newly born atoms are more stable the longer they have cohered, which no one would readily state. But we cannot assign a moment at which the cohesion of two atoms begins, because the whole cohesion is at the same time perfect. And if cohesion does not begin unless it has lasted for some time, it will never begin, for it would be earlier than itself. Moreover, every rest can be understood as composed from two motions, so that if a body is composed from two motions at the same time and therefore rests by accident, will it then also be understood to cling to the walls of the other that it touches? And so wherever we turn, we happen upon absurdities, which is not surprising, because we have assumed an unreasonable hypothesis, namely that the greatest stability has no intelligible cause.

But if anyone at least thinks that atoms can be made by a decree of God, we admit to him that God can bring them about, but a perpetual miracle would be needed so that they resist separation, since a principle of perfect firmness cannot be understood in body itself. God is able to do whatever is possible, but it is not always possible for him to transfer his own power to created things, and for him to bring it about that they can do by themselves what can be achieved only by his power.

2. Whether the essence of body consists in extension (18 June 1691)[8]

If the essence of body consisted in extension, then this extension alone should suffice to explain all the properties of body. But that is not so. We observe in matter a quality that some people have called *natural inertia*, by which body resists motion in some way, such that some force must be employed in order to move it (even leaving aside the weight) and that a large body is more difficult to move than a small body. For example figure 1:

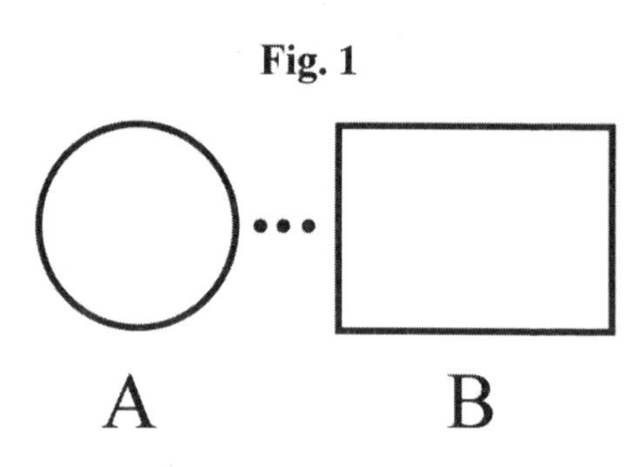

If body A in motion encounters body B at rest, it is clear that if body B were indifferent to motion or rest it would allow itself to be pushed by body A without resisting it, and without diminishing the speed or changing the direction of body A. And after the encounter, A would continue on its path and B would go with it, accompanying it ahead. But it is not that way in nature. The larger the body B, the more it will diminish body A's original speed, to the extent that A is even forced to rebound if B is very much larger than A. Now *if there were nothing in bodies besides extension*, or location, that is to say, besides what geometers know about them, together with the sole notion of change, then this extension would be entirely indifferent with regard to this change, and the results of the encounter of bodies would be explained by the geometric composition of the motions alone. That is to say, *the body after the encounter would always continue with a motion composed of the impulsion that it had before the impact, and the one it would receive from the encountered body in not stopping it*, that is to say, *in this case of collision*, it would move with the difference of the two speeds, and in the direction of the greater speed.

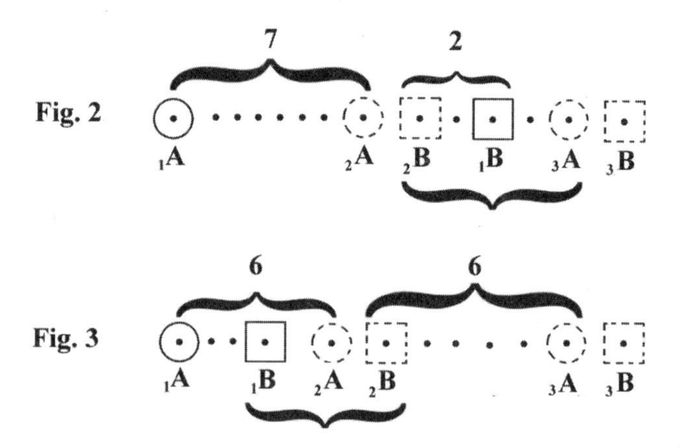

Just as the velocity $_2A\ _3A$, or $_2B\ _3B$, in figure 2, is the difference between $_1A\ _2A$ and $_1B\ _2B$; and in the case of contact, in figure 3, when the fastest would hit the slower one ahead of it, the slowest would receive the speed of the other, and generally they would always proceed together after the encounter; and particularly, as I said at the beginning, the one which is in motion would carry with it the one which is at rest, without receiving any diminution of its speed, and without any change at all arising from the magnitude, equal or unequal, of the two bodies, which is entirely irreconcilable with experience. And although we should suppose that magnitude ought to bring about a change in the motion, we do not have a principle to determine the means of assessing it in detail, and to know the resultant direction and speed. In any case one would incline to the opinion of the conservation of motion, whereas I believe I have demonstrated that the same force is conserved,[9] and that its quantity is different from the quantity of motion. All of this shows that there is in matter something other than what is purely geometric, that is to say, something other than extension and its bare change. And in considering this properly, we see that we must combine some higher or metaphysical notion, namely that of substance, action, and force, and these notions imply that anything which is acted on must act reciprocally, and that anything which acts must suffer some reaction; and consequently a body at rest should not be carried off by another body in motion without changing something of the direction and speed of the acting body. I still agree that naturally every body is extended, and that there is no extension without body. Nevertheless we must not confuse the notions of place, space, or of pure extension with the notion of substance, which, besides extension, includes resistance, that is to say, action and passion. This consideration appears to me important not only in order to know the nature of extended substance, but also in order not to scorn in physics the higher and immaterial principles at the expense of piety. For although I am convinced that everything in corporeal nature happens mechanically, I also continue to believe that the very principles of mechanics, that is to say, the first laws of motion, have a more sublime origin than those that pure mathematics can provide. And I imagine that if that were more widely known, or better considered, many persons of piety would not have so low an opinion of the corpuscular philosophy, and modern philosophers would better combine the knowledge of nature with that of its author. I do not elaborate on other reasons touching on the nature of body, for that would take me too far.

3. Letter to Johann Bernoulli (August–September 1698?)[10]

As for the nature of body, I have often said (and you do not seem to disapprove of it) that all phenomena in bodies can be explained mechanically, and therefore even the force of elasticity can be explained this way. However the actual mechanical principles or the laws of motion cannot be derived from a consideration of extension and impenetrability alone; and so there must be something else in body, the modification of which gives rise to conatus and impetus, just as the modification of extension gives rise to shapes. By 'monad' I understand a substance truly one, namely a substance which is not an aggregate of substances. Matter in itself, or bulk, which you may call primary matter, is not a substance; in fact it is not an aggregate of substances either, but something incomplete. Secondary matter, or mass, is not a substance, but *substances*: so the flock is not one substance, but the animal is; likewise the fish pond is not one substance, but the fish is. But even if the body of an animal, or my organic body, is in turn composed of innumerable substances, they are nevertheless not parts of the animal or of me. But if there were no souls or things analogous to them, then there would be no 'I', no monads, no real unities, and therefore there would be no substantial multitudes; indeed, bodies would be composed entirely of phantasms. From this we can easily judge that there is no part of matter in which monads do not exist.

4. Letter to Burcher de Volder (24 March/3 April 1699)[11]

I do not think that substance consists in extension alone, since the concept of extension is incomplete. Nor do I think that extension can be conceived through itself, but I do think that it is a resolvable and relative concept, since it is resolved into plurality, continuity and co-existence, i.e. the existence of parts at one and the same time. Plurality also belongs to number, and continuity to time and motion, but co-existence consists in extension alone. But even from this it is evident that something must always be supposed which is continued or diffused, as is the whiteness in milk, the colour, ductility and weight in gold, and the resistance in matter. For continuity in itself (for extension is nothing but a simultaneous continuation) no more constitutes a complete substance than does multitude or number, where there must be things that are counted, repeated and continued. And so I believe that our thought of substance is completed and terminated more in the notion of force than in the notion of extension, and no other notion of power or force should be sought than that of an attribute from which change follows, the subject of which is substance itself. I fail to see what is difficult to grasp here. The nature of the idea does not allow a clearer expression, such as a picture. I think that the unity of an extended thing exists only in abstraction, as long as we divert the mind from the internal motion of the parts by which each and every part of matter is in turn actually subdivided into different parts, which even plenitude does not prevent. And the parts of matter do not differ only in their modes, if they are distinguished by souls and entelechies, which always exist.

I have noticed that somewhere in his letters Descartes also recognized inertia in matter,[12] following the example of Kepler. You deduce this inertia from the force which each thing has to persist in its own state, which does not differ from its very own nature. Thus you think that the simple concept of extension is sufficient even for this phenomenon. But the very axiom concerning the conservation of state needs modification, since (for example) what moves in a curved line does not preserve its curvature but only its direction. But if there is a force present in matter for preserving its own state, it certainly cannot be derived in any way from extension alone. I admit that each thing remains in its own state until there is a reason for change, which is a principle of metaphysical necessity; but it is one thing to retain a state until there is something that changes it, which also occurs when a thing is intrinsically indifferent with regard to both states, and another thing, much more significant, when a thing is not indifferent but has a force and as it were an inclination to preserve its own state and thus resist change. And so formerly, in a little book I published when I was a young man, I assumed that matter was intrinsically indifferent to motion and rest, from which I inferred that the largest resting body ought to be moved by the smallest moving body without weakening its motion, and from this I inferred rules of motion abstracted from the system of things.[13] And such a world, in which matter at rest obeys a moving body with any resistance, could indeed be imagined as possible, but it would surely be pure chaos. And so the two tests on which I always depend in such cases – success in experiment and the principle of order – afterwards caused me to recognize that matter was so created by God that a sort of aversion to motion and, in a word, a resistance belongs to it, by which a body intrinsically resists motion, so that when at rest it actually resists motion, but when in motion it resists a greater motion even in the same direction, and in resisting it weakens the force of the moving body.

Therefore since matter intrinsically opposes motion through a general passive force of resistance but is brought to motion through a particular force of activity or entelechy, it follows that inertia also constantly resists through the enduring motion of the entelechy or the motive force. From this I have shown, in a previous letter, that a united force is stronger, i.e. that the force is twice as great if two degrees of speed are united in one pound than if they are divided between two pounds, and that therefore the force of one pound moved with twice the velocity is twice as great as that of two pounds with the simple velocity, because although the quantity of velocity is the same in both cases, the inertia of matter in one pound resists half as much as that of two pounds. The inequality of the forces between one pound and two, both having a velocity inversely proportional to their masses, has been demonstrated in another way from our estimation of forces, but it is also elegantly derived from the consideration of inertia, so well do all things conspire. And so the resistance of matter contains two features: impenetrability, or antitypy, and resistance, or inertia, and since they are everywhere equal in body or proportional to its extension, it is in these features that I locate the nature of the passive principle, or matter, just as in the active force which exercises itself through motion I acknowledge a primitive entelechy and, in a word, something analogous to the soul, whose nature consists in a certain perpetual law of the same series of changes which it traverses unhindered. Nor can we do without this active principle or source of activity, for accidental or changeable active forces and motions themselves are certain modifications of some substantial thing, but forces and actions cannot be modifications of a merely passive thing, as is matter. Therefore it follows that there exists a primary active or substantial thing which is modified by the added disposition of matter, i.e. passivity. Hence, secondary or motive forces and motion itself must be attributed to secondary matter, or to the complete body which results from the active and passive.

5. Letter to Thomas Burnett (2 February 1700)[14]

In bodies I distinguish corporeal substance from matter, and I distinguish primary matter from secondary matter. Secondary matter is an aggregate or composite of several corporeal substances, just as a flock is composed of several animals. But each animal, and each plant too, is a corporeal substance, having in itself a principle of unity, which ensures that it is truly a substance and not an aggregate. And this principle of unity is that which one calls 'soul', or rather that something which has some analogy with the soul. But besides the principle of unity, corporeal substance has its mass or its secondary matter, which is again an aggregate of other, smaller corporeal substances, and that carries on to infinity. However, primitive matter, or matter considered in itself, is what is conceived in bodies considered separately from all the principles of unity; that is to say, it is the passive principle, from which arises two qualities: *resistentia et restitantia vel inertia* [resistance, and obstinacy or inertia]. That is to say that a body does not allow itself to be penetrated, and instead gives way to another, but it does not give way without difficulty and without weakening the total motion of the body that pushes it. Thus it can be said that matter in itself, besides extension, contains a primitive, passive power. But the principle of unity contains a primitive, active power, or the primitive force, which can never be destroyed and always perseveres in the exact order of its internal modifications, which represent those outside it. As a result, that which is essentially passive could not receive the modification of thought without receiving at the same time some substantial active principle which is attached to it; and consequently, matter considered separately could not think, but nothing prevents active principles or principles of unity – which exist everywhere in matter and which already essentially contain a manner of perception – from being elevated to this degree of perception that we call thought. Thus even though matter itself could not think, nothing prevents corporeal substances from thinking.

6. Letter to Burcher de Volder (30 June 1704)[15]

From the very fact that a mathematical body cannot be resolved into primary constituents, we can certainly infer that it is not real, but something mental, designating nothing but the possibility of parts, not anything actual. Indeed, a mathematical line is like arithmetical unity, and in both cases the parts are only possible and completely indefinite. And a line is no more an aggregate of the lines into which it can be divided than a unity is an aggregate of the fractions into which it can be broken up. And as a number that numbers things is not a substance without the things numbered, so a mathematical body, or extension, is not substance without the active and passive, or motion. But in real things, namely bodies, the parts are not indefinite (as they are in space, which is a mental thing), but are actually assigned in a certain way, as nature institutes actual divisions and subdivisions according to the varieties of motions, and although these divisions proceed to infinity, nevertheless all things result from certain primary constituents or real unities, although infinite in number. But strictly speaking, matter is not composed of constitutive unities, but results from them, since matter, i.e. extended mass, is only a phenomenon founded in things, as is a rainbow or parhelion, and all reality exists only in unities. Therefore phenomena can always be divided into lesser phenomena, which can be seen by other, subtler animals, and we will never arrive at the least phenomena. But substantial unities are not parts, only the foundations of phenomena.

B. The Laws of Nature

1. On a general principle useful in explaining the laws of nature through a consideration of the divine wisdom, to serve as a reply to Father Malebranche's response (July 1687)[16]

I have seen, in the *Nouvelles de la République des Lettres*, Malebranche's reply to the remark I made on some laws of nature that he had established in the *Search after Truth*. He seems sufficiently disposed to abandon them himself, and this ingenuousness is highly commendable; but as he gives reasons and restrictions, which would bring us back into the obscurity from which I believe I have freed this subject, and which are at odds with a principle of general order that I have observed, I hope that he will have the kindness to permit me to use this opportunity to explain this principle, which is of great use in reasoning and which I do not yet find sufficiently employed nor sufficiently known in all its extent. It has its origin in the infinite, it is absolutely necessary in geometry, but it also holds in physics, because the sovereign wisdom, which is the source of all things, acts as a perfect geometrician, and according to a harmony to which nothing can be added. This is why this principle often serves as a proof or test to show from the outset and from the outside the error of a badly devised opinion, even before coming to an internal discussion. It can be expressed thus: *when the difference of two cases can be diminished below any magnitude given in the data or in what is posited, it must also be found diminished below any magnitude given in what is sought or in what results from it,* or to speak more familiarly: *when the cases (or data), continually approach each other and one finally merges into the other, then the results or outcomes (or what is required) must do likewise.* This depends again on a more general principle, namely: *datis ordinatis etiam quaesita sunt ordinata* [when the data are ordered, the things sought are ordered too]. But in order to understand it examples are needed. It is known that the case or the supposition of an ellipse may approach the case of a parabola as much as we like, so much so that the difference of the ellipse and of the parabola can become less than any given difference, provided that one of the foci of the ellipse is sufficiently distant from the other, for then the radii coming from this distant focus will differ from the parallel radii as little as we like, and consequently all the geometrical theorems which are verified of the ellipse in general can be applied to the parabola, by considering the latter as an ellipse, one of the foci of which is infinitely distant, or (to avoid this expression) as a shape which differs from some ellipse by less than any given difference. The same principle holds good in physics; for example, rest can be considered as an infinitely small velocity, or as an infinite slowness. This is why everything that is true as regards slowness or velocity in general should also be confirmed of rest taken in this way; so much so that the rule of rest should be considered as a particular case of the rule of motion: otherwise, if this does not hold, it will be a sure sign that the rules are badly devised. Likewise equality can be considered as an infinitely small inequality, and inequality can be made to approach equality as much as we like.

It is, among other errors, concerning this consideration that Mr Descartes, very clever man that he was, failed in more than one way in his so-called laws of nature. For (not to repeat now what I said before of the other source of his errors, when he took the quantity of motion for force) his first and his second rule, for example, do not agree with each other. The second claims if that two bodies B and C collide in a straight line with equal velocities, and B is larger by as little as possible, C will be deflected with its initial velocity, but B will continue its movement, whereas according to the first law, if B and C are equal, they will both be deflected and turn back with a velocity equal to that which had brought them together.[17] But the difference between the outcomes of these two cases is not reasonable; for as the inequality of the two bodies can be as small as we like, and the difference in the suppositions of these two cases, namely the difference between such inequality and a perfect equality, could be less than any given, then in accordance with our principle the difference between the results or outcomes should also be less than any given; nevertheless if the second rule were true as well as the first, the contrary would happen, for according to this second rule an increase as small as we like in body B, beforehand being equal to C, makes a tremendous difference in the outcome, such that it changes absolute deflection into absolute continuation, which is a great leap from one extreme to the other, whereas in this case body B should deflect a little bit less, and body C a little bit more than in the case of equality, from which this case can hardly be distinguished.

There are several other incongruities like this which result from the Cartesian rules, which the attention of a reader applying our principle will easily notice, and the one that I found in the rules of the *Search after Truth* came from the same source. Reverend Father Malebranche admits in some way that there are inconsistencies in them, but he continues to believe that laws of motion, which depend on the good pleasure of God, could be established as irregular as these ones. But the good pleasure of God is regulated by his wisdom, and geometricians would be almost as surprised to see these sorts of irregularities happen in nature as to see a parabola to which the properties of an ellipse with an infinitely distant focus could not be applied. Thus the example of such inconsistencies will never be encountered in nature, I think, since the more she is known the more she is found to be geometrical. It is easy to judge from this that these inconsistencies do not properly come from what Reverend Father Malebranche suggests they do, namely from the false hypothesis of the perfect hardness of bodies, which I admit is not found in nature. For even if we were to suppose this hardness in it, by regarding it as infinitely quick elasticity, nothing would result from it which should not adjust perfectly to the true laws of nature as regards elastic bodies in general, and we shall never come to rules as inconsistent as those that I have found fault with.

It is true that in composite things sometimes a little change can bring about a great effect, as, for example, a spark falling into a great mass of gunpowder is capable of overturning a whole city. But this is not contrary to our principle, since it can be explained by the same general principles, but as regards rudimentary or simple things, nothing similar could happen, otherwise nature would not be the effect of infinite wisdom. By this we see, a little better than in what is commonly said about it, how true physics should in fact be derived from the source of the divine perfections. It is God who is the final reason of things, and the knowledge of God is no less the principle of the sciences than his essence and his will are the principles of beings. The most reasonable philosophers remain agreed on this, but there are very few of them who can make use of it to discover important truths. Perhaps these little examples will arouse some to go much further. It is sanctifying philosophy to make its streams flow from the fountain of God's attributes. Far from excluding final causes and the consideration of a being acting with wisdom, it is from there that everything must be deduced in physics. This is what Socrates, in Plato's *Phaedo*, has already admirably remarked, when reasoning against Anaxagoras and other overly materialistic philosophers who, after having at first recognized an intelligent principle above matter, do not employ it at all when they come to philosophize about the universe, and instead of showing that this intelligence does everything for the best and that this is the reason of the things that it found good to produce in accordance with its ends, try to explain everything by the collision of brute particles alone, thus confusing the conditions and instruments with the true cause.[18] It is (says Socrates) as if, in order to explain why I am seated in prison awaiting the fatal cup and am not on the way to the Boeotians or other peoples, where we know I could have saved myself, it should be said that it is because I have bones, tendons and muscles which can bend as required in order to be seated. Well (he says), these bones and these muscles would not be here, and you would not see me in this posture, if my mind had not judged that it is more worthy of Socrates to be subjected to what the laws of the country ordain. This passage in Plato deserves to be read in its entirety, for these are very beautiful and very sound reflections. Nevertheless I grant that particular effects of nature could and should be explained mechanically, though without forgetting their admirable ends and uses which providence has known how to organize. But the general principles of physics and even of mechanics depend on the conduct of a sovereign intelligence, and cannot be explained without taking it into consideration. It is in this way that piety should be reconciled with reason, and that good people may be satisfied who fear the results of the mechanical or corpuscular philosophy, as if it would take us away from God and immaterial substances, whereas with the required corrections and everything well understood, it ought to lead us to them.

2. Letter to Pierre Bayle (1702?)[19]

If my thinking about force can give some satisfaction to you, Sir, and a small number of people like you, I will be quite happy with that. Perhaps the clarification that I will give here will satisfy you still more. In the past, my first consideration was that there ought to be conserved in nature something that always produces an equal effect; for example when several bodies collide, on a horizontal plane if you will, and no part of the force is absorbed by friction, by the environment or by the insensible parts of bodies, I judged that it was necessary that all of them together would always be capable by their impulsions of raising the same weight to the same height, or of bending springs to certain determined degrees, or to give certain velocities to certain bodies. But in examining that closely, I found that this conservation of force did not agree at all with that of the quantity of motion, which appeared to me to rely on a reason that was too vague, whereas the conservation of force was confirmed by experience and by a constant reason of the absurdity of perpetual mechanical motion; that, together with many other considerations, prevented me from balancing this force and the state from which action follows. But as you take it, Sir, as if I mean a striving in bodies which do not change place, which is equivalent to the activity of the translation from place to place, I see that I need to explain myself and to say that I believe that force is always accompanied by an action and even a local motion, which can correspond to it.

Nevertheless it is not the quantity of this motion but the quantity of force which is conserved; almost as when two globes are combined, the sum of the two surfaces is not conserved but that of solidities, even though solidities are never without suitable surfaces. But now here is what completes the resolution of the difficulty. It came about through a new approach, which taught me that not only is the same force conserved, but also the same quantity of motive action, which is different from that of motion, as you will see by an argument with which I myself was surprised, since no one has made so easy a remark on a matter so well worn. Here is my argument: In the uniform motion of a single body (1) the action of traversing two leagues in two hours is double the action of traversing one league in one hour (since the first action contains the second precisely two times); (2) the action of traversing one league in one hour is double the action of traversing one league in two hours (or rather, actions which produce the same effect are proportional to their speeds). Therefore (3) the action of traversing two leagues in two hours is four times the action of traversing one league in two hours. This demonstration shows that a moving body receiving a double or triple speed so as to be able to produce a double or triple effect in the same time, receives an action four or nine times as great. Thus, actions are proportional to the square of the speeds. Now most fortunately it is found that this agrees with my estimate of force, drawn either from experience or from the basis of the avoidance of perpetual mechanical motion. For according to my estimate, forces are proportional to the heights from which heavy bodies might descend in order to acquire these speeds, that is to say, proportional to the square of speeds. And as the force is always conserved in order to raise something finally to the same height or to produce some other effect, it follows that the same quantity of motive action is also conserved in the world; that is, in order to get it right, there is in one hour as much motive action in the universe as there is in any other hour whatsoever. So the intention of our philosophers, and particularly of the late Mr Descartes, was good in conserving action and in estimating the force by the action; but they have taken a *quid pro quo* by taking what they call the quantity of motion for the quantity of motive action. There are very few people to whom I have revealed this argument, not wishing to prostitute it before those who have no taste for abstract thoughts. I say nothing here about the respective forces and actions which are also conserved and have their own separate estimations; and there are many other marvellous equalities or conservations, which show not only the constancy but also the perfection of the author of the world.

3. Letter to Bernard le Bovier de Fontenelle (7 April 1703)[20]

As for the laws of motion, they can be demonstrated by making certain suppositions, but each has something that is independent of geometric necessity, and that depends on the principle of fittingness or perfection. Mr Huygens proposes the principle of the boat, that is to say of equivalence, as regards the impact of bodies; between a body, for example, truly at rest and without action, and a body that moves from the bow to the stern at a speed equal to that of the boat, which makes it seem as if this body is at rest to the eyes of the spectator on the banks of the canal. This remark fortunately agrees with experience but one could not demonstrate the necessity of it.

You ask, Sir, if the laws of motion are indifferent to the nature of matter. I reply Yes, if you oppose 'indifferent' to 'necessary', and I reply No if you oppose it to 'fitting'; that is to say, if you oppose it to what is the best and gives the most perfection. It is the same if you talk of 'arbitrary'. These laws are not as arbitrary or indifferent as some have believed, nor as necessary as others have believed. Thus the laws of motion are no more geometrically necessary than is architecture. And nevertheless there are between them and the nature of body relations that indeed do not escape us completely. These relations are founded principally in the entelechy or principle of force which joined to matter results in complete corporeal substance. It can even be said that these laws are naturally essential to this entelechy or primitive force that God has put into bodies, and consequently into corporeal substance; for if they did not originate from that they would not be natural at all, but miraculous, and God would be obliged to achieve observance of them by a continual miracle. But they are not essential to matter at all, that is to say to what is passive in corporeal substance.

We could invent many other laws, and to say nothing of those of Descartes or of the *Search after Truth*,[21] I have formerly demonstrated and repeated in a few words in one of the *Journal des Savants* how things should happen naturally in collision if there were in bodies only matter or passiveness,[22] which is to say extension and impenetrability, but these laws are not compatible with ours and would produce the most absurd and irregular effects in the world, and would violate amongst other things the law of continuity that I believe I was the first to introduce, and which is also not altogether of geometric necessity, as when it decrees that there is no change *by a leap*. Thus we should not imagine that there is some world in which these laws that follow from pure materiality obtain, or others just as unfitting as they are. In the same way, we should not believe with Lucretius that there are worlds in which, instead of animals, the collision of atoms forms detached arms or legs, nor finally that everything possible occurs however unreasonable it may be, or to want it to belong to the greatness and magnificence of God that he should make everything that is possible. Apart from the fact that this is impossible, because of the incompatibility of possibles and the connection of all creatures; quite apart from that, it is, I say, to want grandeur at the expense of beauty. And it is as if, pretending that it was one of the perfections of God to be a poet, we wanted this perfect poet to produce all possible verses, good and bad; the same applies to an architect, and God truly is one.

Only the essence of God is necessary, and it implies contradiction that it does not exist. But God is determined to produce other beings not by the law of necessity, as would be true if he produced everything possible, but by the law of wisdom or the law of the best, of the best ordered, of the most perfect.

C. Biology[23]

1. On the origin of fossils (late 1670s?)[24]

I have difficulty believing that the bones that are sometimes found in fields, or that are discovered while digging in the earth, are the remains of true giants: likewise, that the stones of Malta, which are so commonly called snake tongues, are parts of fish: and that the shells which are buried quite far from the sea are certain signs that the sea covered these places and that it left these shells as it withdrew, and that they have subsequently been petrified.

If that were so, the earth would have to be much older than the holy histories suggest: but I do not want to dwell on this; we are concerned here with using natural grounds. I therefore believe that the forms of these animal bones and shells are often merely tricks of nature, which have been formed separately, without coming from animals. For it is well known that stones grow and assume a thousand strange forms: witness the stone figures collected by the Reverend Father Kircher in his *Subterranean World*.[25] It is likewise known that plants very often take the form of animals or their parts; witness the mandrake and several others which could be collected. Indeed, it should not be imagined that in animals themselves the parts form by means of a soul or some mysterious principle; on the contrary, I believe that this happens by purely mechanical reasons, and if they are known in detail as good a reason would be given for these figures as for that of a sugarloaf or a hat. That is why these same mechanical reasons, being able to be found outside of an animal, will give the same shape to a sap which has solidified. This is so obvious that I would be surprised if it did not occur on occasion.

In my view, this opinion has no difficulties, whereas the contrary suffers from great difficulties from history as well as reason. For the shells that are claimed to be petrified are sometimes found in rocks which are drawn from mountains that are rather high. Now how likely is it that the sea covered these mountains for a considerable time, as we must suppose here? For as the sea seeks its own level, it must be that all of it was as high everywhere. That being so, it is right to ask what has become of this phenomenal quantity of water. It is not very likely that a great part of the sea and the land was consumed and dissipated by time, and that these wretched shells escaped from such a great change. I add that rock shells of several unknown species are found that one will seek in vain in the sea, a sign that these are tricks of nature, unless it is maintained that these species have been lost, which is not likely. Moreover, such a great quantity of shells and so-called fish bones are found piled up on top of one another that there is much more reason to believe that the Earth, in those places, had in it some particular force to produce them in such great quantity, than to imagine that the sea carried so many of them to the same place; since one would have much difficulty nowadays finding such great pieces in the sea itself. There is still one matter to consider, which is that these bones are sometimes so big that it is not credible that the animals were proportionally as big. To prove that, I remember that St. Augustine said that he had seen in Utica, in Africa, a tooth so big that if it had been cut into small pieces it seemed that it could have made a hundred of ours.[26] But it is not very credible that there ever were giants a hundred times bigger than us. For according to Galileo's reasonings, the size of animals must have limits, unless nature makes them from another kind of material which has more firmness and strength than ours. And it is for this reason that the biggest aquatic animals surpass by far the biggest among the terrestrials, and that there is no comparison at all between a whale and an elephant, since bodies weigh less in water than in air, as can be easily proved when being in the bath, for the arms can be raised almost without any effort when they are under water; this is why the movement of aquatic animals is proportionally easier, the parts of their body are more responsive, and their weight makes it easier for them to be coordinated. Thus aquatic animals can be bigger than terrestrial ones. All these reasons tell against these huge giants, and others will doubtless be found in Riolan's *Gigantology* that I remember having seen.[27] But without dwelling on this question, and even if we remain agreed that there were tremendous giants, I nevertheless maintain that most of the so-called bones of terrestrial animals or fish, which are believed to have been petrified some thousands of years ago, are only true rocks perhaps formed not long ago by the plastic power of the Earth. It has happened to me more than once while travelling that I have noticed fields completely covered with rocks, which were very similar to the bones of animals, and country folk would swear that although these fields were cleared up from time to time, these same rocks would not fail to return. To cap off all these reasons I add to them one which would be strong if it was confirmed, which is that I believe I have heard that shells have been found in a rock created inside the body of an animal. Nevertheless, to show that I am fair-minded, I admit that we should say that these rocks were at some point parts of animals in cases where a too perfect resemblance is found, which could not be the effect of chance.

2. Protogaea (selections) (1691–1693)[28]

§6 . . . There are those who go so far in their bold conjecturing as to think that all animals, which now dwell on the Earth, were covered by the sea, and have at some time been aquatic, and little by little, deserting their element, became amphibious and finally in succeeding generations forgot their first home. But aside from the fact that such a view disagrees with the Holy writers, to depart from whom is a religious offence, the hypothesis suffers from immense difficulties in itself . . .

§25 The shells and bones of marine animals that are dug up can be examined and explained just as well as the parts of real animals.

The more closely you examine the actual parts of bodies, the fewer doubts you will have about their origin. For they are not resistant to examination, like those amusing imitations in marble of men or houses which one has to observe from a distance. A more careful analysis will show that the shellfish of the shore, no less than those found in rock, have the same kind of texture consisting of hard parts and fibres, and what appears to be seams, and are divided into cells, and also they can be dissolved in vinegar (that is, whenever they are covered rather than impregnated by the stony material), and sometimes pearls are discovered within, and the animal itself is preserved in its own shell of stone as if in balsam. Finally, near Volterra in Tuscany, and near Reggio in Calabria, are found in the layers of the earth unmistakable shells displaying no change at all, and without any petrification. Similarly, the remains of animals are dug up near to us, from the mud in a cave near Scharzfeld, which is called by the inhabitants the cave of the Pygmies. Therefore there is no reason why we should conclude the origin is different when the earth has turned to stone.

§26 In very ancient times the nearby seas contained animals and molluscs that are not found there now.

That which learned men otherwise urge, scarcely undermines the argument. They have difficulty convincing themselves that the sea has been in the highest mountains, or that things of the sea have existed there: evidently because they judge the former appearance of the world too much by its present appearance, and every flood they look to explain simply by the rains, not sufficiently considering that sometimes the waters of the great abyss have burst through and overflowed. Others are amazed that species can be seen everywhere in stones, which you may look for in vain either in the known world, or at least in nearby places. Thus they say that ammonites, which may be considered to be from the nautilus species, differ everywhere both in form and magnitude (for sometimes they are even discovered measuring a foot in diameter) from all those which now live in the sea. But who has fully explored its hidden recesses, or the subterranean abysses? How many animals, previously unknown to us, does the new world offer? It is quite credible that during those great changes the species of animals have still remained mostly unchanged. Lachmund illustrates our ammonites in fossils from our country, from where we have copied out the illustrations here. But a careful investigator of the works of nature, the Englishman John Ray, has inquired more fully into these matters. And I do not doubt that through such a great disturbance of things that the spoils of the sea are often brought from distant shores, since now it is also agreed that everywhere storms throw up kinds of molluscs onto our coasts which fishermen do not find in the nearby sea. And when a huge mass of similar things have collected in one place, such as in Malta alone we wonder at the huge number of shark's teeth which are called glossopetrae,[29] it is not foolish to attribute it to the whirlpools of the seas, where after much agitation, the result has been that they have deposited in one particular place through a combination of their movement and weight. In short, it is just as in the crystallization of different salts dissolved in the same liquid, when we see salts joining with similar salts without mingling. For the most part, as I believe, water, finding its way through narrow places, has abandoned what it was carrying. The inevitable result has been that a huge mass of things from the sea has soon been accumulated, always in an unusual manner, and by a flood tide laden with flotsam before it passes into narrow places.

3. Letter from G. W. Leibniz (1710)[30]

To the author of the dissertation on the shapes of animals which are observed in rocks, and that may be called by the name 'zoolithes'.

Most distinguished and respected Sir,
I greatly applaud your crocodile fossil, and I am delighted that having yielded to my encouragement you have finished the dissertation on it that you had contemplated. You know that I am of the same opinion; to some extent the mineral impression has taken, as it were, the actual place of the real crocodile. I have broadly put forth my judgement on this many years ago, in a dissertation not yet published, *On the vestiges of ancient history in the monuments of nature itself.* I have even indicated some thoughts in passing in a summary I formerly placed in the *Acts of Leipzig*, under the title *Protogaea*, such as a conjecture concerning a lake or a receptacle of waters buried by the earth, and the fish found there, like those in Eisleben, and if you do not find this entirely satisfactory, nevertheless I think that it is not to be altogether scorned. For the fish there, as in Osterode, at the base of our Harz Mountains (I believe also elsewhere) are discovered in a sloping stratum or almost approaching the horizontal; one may reason from this that the fish formerly lived in generally the same horizontal plane, that is, in some lake.[31] Moreover, I tend to believe that, just as certain things followed the flood of Noah, so many other things preceded it. For many things lead me to think that it is consistent with reason and with Holy Scripture itself, that the whole globe of the earth before the birth of man was at some point covered by the sea, at the time when God ordered the waters to withdraw from the land; and earlier still it was consumed by fire, at the time when he separated the light from the darkness; and afterwards other great changes followed, of which we suspect nothing today. As for the animals unknown in this world, of which we have discovered vestiges, further enquiry must be made as to whether or not the majority were aquatic or amphibious; especially since it can be believed that some terrestrial animals have ultimately descended from marine or amphibious animals which have now been deserted by the sea, and which have

changed over a long period of time so that they can no longer bear the water. I once showed Mr Tentzel, of pious memory, the remains of an animal dug up from a stone quarry near Wolfenbüttel; in particular a part of a jawbone with teeth, which resembles an animal not unlike the elephant, but nevertheless different.[32] I could not determine if it was terrestrial or aquatic; and I would certainly not deny that terrestrial animals have been carried to distant shores and piled up elsewhere by the force of the waters; since a great quantity of the water could flow into certain kinds of fissures, by which it was perhaps admitted into the internal cavities of the earth, such as Lucian describes regarding the cave of Hierapolis.[33] I even believe that kinds of terrestrial animals that formerly lived on our shores have today perished, whether on account of a climatic change, or on account of other reasons that would be difficult to guess, because of the obscurity of remote matters. Moreover, the observation of our Scheuchzer (that distinguished man of outstanding merit in natural history), that you quote, on the images of plants in relief that can be seen in rocks, pleases me greatly, for it resembles a genuine plant in the smallest detail so that it can hardly be doubted that it is an impression of one. Mr Heinius asks us to hope for a complete subterranean botany from rocks, since he discovered plants of the Indies in the mines of Saxony. And although he has brought forward many ingenious arguments, and suggests that it should be further considered whether or not they may be accounted for by what the vulgar call 'tricks of nature' – and I would not deny this in some cases – nevertheless in many cases the sheer accuracy of these forms proves that a different judgement should be made. Farewell.

Notes

1 See also I.B.5, II.A.4.
2 G VII 284–8. Latin.
3 Leibniz wrote in the margin here: 'Whatever is distinguishable through itself is also distinguishable extrinsically. If two bodies are alike in comparison with a third body, they cannot be distinguished. If two bodies are alike but are not in themselves equal to each other, they cannot be distinguished extrinsically, not even in comparison with an assumed third body. Bodies extrinsically similar and equal cannot be distinguished in any way, and are truly one and the same.'
4 Presumably a slip for '*D*'.
5 Reading *ostendimus* for *ostendinus*.
6 Gerhardt notes that the remainder of this sentence is illegible.
7 Leibniz wrote in the margin here: 'Another such argument could be established on these lines: if there be atoms, then bodies similar and equal but different from each other could exist, so that there could be two equal spheres.'
8 E 112–13. French. Originally published in the *Journal des Savants*.
9 'A brief demonstration of a notable error of Descartes and others concerning a natural law' (1686), in L 296–302.
10 GM III 536–7. Latin.
11 G II 169–71. Latin.
12 See, for example, Descartes' letter to Mersenne of 25 December 1639 in volume II of C. Adam and P. Tannery (eds), *Oeuvres de Descartes*, Paris: Vrin, p. 627.
13 *Theory of Abstract Motion* (1671), in L 139–42.
14 A I xviii 375–6. French.

15 G II 268. Latin.
16 G III 51–5. French.
17 Descartes, *Principles of Philosophy*, part II, arts 46 and 47.
18 Plato, *Phaedo* 97b9–99b6.
19 G III 58–61. French.
20 FC 225–8. French.
21 Nicolas Malebranche.
22 A reference to 'Whether the essence of body consists in extension', pp. 123–5 of this volume.
23 See also II.C.2.
24 LH 37, 4 Ff 14r–15v. French.
25 Athanasius Kircher, *Subterranean World* (1665).
26 St. Augustine, *City of God*, book 15, chapter 9.
27 Jean Riolan, *Gigantology* (1618).
28 D II 205, 220–1. Latin.
29 Literally 'tongue stones'.
30 D II 176–7. Latin. Originally published in the journal *Miscellanea Berolinensia ad incrementum scientiarum* [*Berlin Miscellanea for the advancement of the sciences*], 118–20. The piece is an open letter addressed to Christian Maximilian Spener, author of the dissertation *Inquiry concerning a crocodile impressed in rock and other zoolithes*, which was published in the same volume of *Berlin Miscellanea* as Leibniz's congratulatory letter.
31 Leibniz proposed this theory in §20 of the *Protogaea*: 'Fish expressed in slate are from true fish, and this proves that they are not tricks of nature . . . Both the multitude of fish contained in one and the same place, and the fact that nothing is there except fish, support my opinion. As for the pontifical crown, Luther, and I do not know what other forms people mention that are delineated in the rock of Eisleben, I regard these truly as tricks, not of nature but of human imagination, which sees armies in the haze, and recognizes in the strokes of bells or drums whatever modulations it wants. And many things are of this kind, which are exhibited to the public in the cave of Baumann, namely Moses and the ascension of Christ, and other images from stone, which you wouldn't recognize unless you were warned. The splendour of things increases according to one's faith in the miraculous, but while I seem to have said that we must be astounded about marvels from our regions, that is not my own belief. But faith is greatest and undoubted in the representation of the fish of Osterode and Eisleben, and one must immediately acknowledge not only the fish but also the genus of the fish and the true size and symmetry of its parts, and the scales, and everything else. The composition of the area itself constitutes a great argument. For we have said that there is a sloping vein of slate containing fish (if I may speak in the terminology of our miners); that is, in a nearly horizontal stratum jutting out by several miles, as is now readily

apparent, the fish of the same lake were pressed by a mass falling on top of them. Sizeable lakes certainly exist even now in the vicinity of Eisleben. And there you can marvel at marine fish in rock, not far from Seeburg, where there is a vast lake of salt water; and fountains of salt waters show that there are repositories of salt under the Earth, of which the most famous is the one that flows from Halle, in Saxony, eight miles from Eisleben, which some have supposed was once the cause of war between the Chatti and the Hermundures.' D II 216–17.

32 Compare Leibniz's letter to Thomas Burnett, 17/27 July 1696: 'In Tonna, near Gotha in Thüringen, some parts of a skeleton were found, which is of an elephant according to all appearances. Some doctors from there claimed that it is a production of the Earth, a trick of nature. I was consulted, and I said that I had no doubt at all that it is from the animal kingdom, and if it is not from an elephant it is still from an analogous animal, either from elephants or similar animals that have formerly lived in these countries, or that there were amphibious sea animals of the nature of the elephant when a large part of the globe of the Earth was still submerged: for species can be greatly changed by length of time, just as by the interval of places, witness the differences between American animals and ours. We have found teeth in Wolfenbüttel that also match those of the elephant, and there are many other examples.' A I xii 735.

33 Lucian, *On the Syrian Goddess*, II.13.

V. LAW AND ETHICS

A. Law

1. Preface to the *Diplomatic Code of People's Rights* (1693)[1]

I am not sure, even after the efforts of so many illustrious writers, that the concepts of law and justice have been made sufficiently clear. *Right* is a kind of moral power, and *obligation* is a moral necessity. I understand *moral*, however, as that which is equivalent to 'natural' for a good man: for as a Roman jurisconsult has famously said, we should believe that we are not able to do that which is contrary to good morals. A good man is one who loves everyone, so far as reason permits. *Justice*, then, is the virtue governing that affection which the Greeks call *philanthropy*, and we shall most fittingly define it, if I am not mistaken, as *the charity* of the wise man, that is, charity following the dictates of wisdom. Therefore what Carneades is supposed to have said, that justice is supreme folly because it commands us to consider the interests of others while ignoring our own, is born out of ignorance of its definition. *Charity* is universal benevolence, and benevolence is the habit of loving or esteeming. But to love or to esteem is to be delighted by the happiness of another, or what amounts to the same, to make the happiness of another into one's own. This resolves the knotty problem, which is also of great importance in theology, of how there can be a disinterested love which is separate from hope and fear and every consideration of utility. Of course the happiness of those whose happiness enters into our own pleases us, for things that delight are desired for their own sake. And just as the contemplation of beautiful things is pleasant in itself, and a painting of Raphael affects the one who understands it, even if it brings him no material gain, so that he keeps it in sight and delights in it, in a kind of image of love, so when the beautiful thing is at the same time also capable of happiness, the affection passes over into pure love. The *divine love*, however, surpasses other loves, because God can be loved with the greatest result, since nothing is happier than God and also nothing can be understood as being more beautiful or more worthy of happiness. And since he also possesses supreme power and supreme wisdom, his happiness does not merely enter into ours (if we are wise, that is, if we love him), but even constitutes it. But because wisdom ought to guide charity, we also need its definition. I believe, however, that we can best satisfy the concept men have of it if we say that *wisdom* is nothing other than the science of happiness itself. So we come round again to the concept of happiness, although this is not the place to explain it.

Now from this source flows *natural right*, of which there are three degrees: *strict right* in commutative justice, *equity* (or charity in the narrower sense of the term) in distributive justice, and finally *piety* (or probity) in universal justice; hence emerges the same number of most general and commonly recognized precepts of right: to injure no one, to give to each his due, and to live honourably (or rather piously), just as I once outlined as a young man in a small book called *On the Method of Right*. The precept of mere right or strict right is that no one is to be injured, so that he is not given grounds for legal action within the state or the right of war outside the state. Hence there arises the justice that philosophers call commutative, and the right that Grotius calls a legal claim.[2] The higher degree I call equity or, if you prefer, charity (that is, in the narrower sense) which I extend beyond the rigour of mere right to include also those obligations, the performance of which gives to those whom they affect no grounds for legal action by which we would be compelled to do them, such as gratitude and alms-giving, to which, according to Grotius, we have a moral claim but not a legal claim.[3] And as the lowest degree of right was to injure no one, so that of the middle degree was to benefit all, but only as far as befits each person or as much as each deserves, since it is not right to favour everyone equally. And so here is found distributive justice and the precept of right which commands that we give to each his due. And it is to here that the political laws of a republic can be traced back, laws which procure the happiness of its subjects and which make it the case everywhere that they who have only a moral claim acquire a legal claim, that is, so that they are able to demand what is equitable for others to perform. And while in the lowest degree of right the differences among men are not considered, except those which arise in each case, but all men are considered equal, now however in this higher degree merits are weighed, and hence privileges, rewards and punishments have their place. The difference in the degrees of right was elegantly outlined by Xenophon in his example of the boy Cyrus, who was chosen to judge between two boys, the stronger of whom had forcibly exchanged coats with the other because he discovered that the other's garment was more suited to his own size and his own garment was more suited to the size of the other boy. Cyrus pronounced in favour of the robber, but was admonished by his master that it was not a question of who the garment fitted but of whose it was, and that he might more properly use this form of judgement only when he himself had coats to distribute.[4] For indeed equity itself recommends strict right, that is the equality of men, in our affairs, except when an important consideration of a greater good commands us to withdraw from it. What is called respect of persons, however, has its place not in exchanging goods with others, but in distributing our own or public goods.

The highest degree of right I have called by the name of probity or rather piety. For until now what has been said can be interpreted in such a way as to be confined to the consideration for mortal life. And indeed mere right or strict right arises from the principle of the preservation of peace; equity or charity extends to something greater, namely that while each benefits others as much as he is able, he may increase his own happiness in that of another. And to say it in a word, while strict right avoids misery, the higher right tends towards happiness, but happiness such as occurs in this mortal life. But that we should esteem this life and everything which makes this life desirable less than the great interest of others, so that we ought to bear the greatest pains for the sake of others, this is taught in the fine words of philosophers rather than proved by solid demonstrations. For the dignity and glory and the joyful feeling in the virtue of one's own mind, to which they appeal under the name of honour, are evidently goods of thought or goods of the mind, and great ones indeed but not overcoming all nor all the severity of evils, since not all men are equally affected by the imagination; especially those whom neither a liberal education nor a noble way of living, or a disciple of life or of a sect, has accustomed to the estimation of honour or to the experience of the goods of the mind. But to accomplish by a universal demonstration that everything honourable is useful and that everything base is harmful, the immortality of the soul and God as ruler of the universe must be assumed. Because of this we realize that we live in the most perfect state, under a monarch who cannot be deceived on account of his wisdom nor evaded on account of his power, and is also so worthy of love that to serve such a master is happiness. Therefore he who expends his soul for him, because of Christ's teaching wins it back. His power and providence makes it so that every right passes over into fact, so that no one is injured except by himself, that nothing done rightly is without reward, and no sin is without punishment. Because, as is divinely related by Christ, all our hairs are numbered, and not even a drink of water is given to the thirsty in vain; indeed nothing is neglected in the state of the universe. From this consideration it comes about that justice is called universal and includes all other virtues, for what does not seem to be otherwise of concern to others, such as not to abuse our own bodies or our own property, even though these things are beyond human laws they are prohibited by natural right, that is, by the eternal laws of the divine monarchy, since we owe ourselves and our goods to God. For as it concerns the state that no one misuses his own property, so it concerns the universe much more. And so it is from this that the highest precept of the law receives its power, which commands us to live honourably (that is, piously). And it is in this sense that it is rightly mentioned by learned men that, among desirable things, the law of nature and of nations should be propounded according to the teaching of Christianity, that is (from the examples of Christ), the sublime things, the divine things of the wise. Thus it seems that we have explained, in the most fitting way, the three precepts of right, or the three degrees of justice, and indicated the origins of natural right.

2. On the death penalty (after 10 July 1697)[5]

The question is whether there are grounds for capital punishment if two witnesses are brought forward against a defendant, witnesses which in a civil case would be considered sufficiently trustworthy to warrant a conviction even though the defendant may firmly deny that he committed the crime.

I believe it to be against both custom and the rule of law, and in such a case the defendant should, depending on the circumstances, only be subjected either to temporal punishment or to torture in order to obtain a confession, and through a lucid and consistent confession a greater light may be obtained, by which the defendant can be so much the more safely convicted.

For as far as custom is concerned, it is clear that defendants in Germany and Italy are rarely accustomed to being convicted without a confession or proofs as clear as the midday sun (which should not only take the form of a simple proof but should contain evidence and should to a certain extent be close to an indictment). Nevertheless I except military crimes and other cases where the necessity of discipline or public utility demands greater severity.

And while I think that the rationality of the law is clear, greater caution is needed with criminal cases, where life is at stake, than in civil cases. And more certainty will be required to impose capital punishment than to order a fine, for it is better (aside from a case of public danger) that the guilty be absolved than the innocent[6] be condemned, and surely the word of two witnesses in a matter of such importance is very unreliable, for what is easier than that two men should conspire to defraud a single person, especially since perjuries and witnesses procured by money are today too widespread. And one may not always be able to distinguish a good man from a crooked man by outward appearance. No prudent person will doubt that such evidence is certainly not as clear as the midday sun, and a great many doubts remain with it. And it is evident that it is from this principle that so many perjuries and convictions of the innocent have recently occurred in England.

Some people mention, not very aptly, the passage of Deuteronomy 19,[7] that the truth is established *in the words of two or three witnesses*, for if that were to be accepted crudely it would follow in criminal cases that not even the substance of an offence is needed for conviction.

Likewise the *Carolina* ordination does not oppose it,[8] for even if article 22 says that the one who admits a crime must be guilty, or rather convicted, it is nevertheless understood that he is to be convicted not by common proofs that are sufficient in civil cases, but by the clearer proofs required for a capital crime matter and so that no one prudent can be in doubt, just as if someone is discovered in the very act of wrongdoing or there are very persuasive circumstances, which support the words of the witnesses.[9]

And what the *Carolina* article 67 says does not contradict this, that with the offence proved by two or three witnesses, the accused can be punished in a criminal trial,[10] and article 69, that the convicted defendant is not to be tortured pointlessly.[11] For the aforesaid article 67 rightly adds the condition that from the testimony of witnesses the defendant can be condemned. *Nach gestalt der Verhandelung* [According to the nature of the case], this is 'according to the quality and measure of the actions and the proofs', and therefore the defendant will be able to be condemned from the words of two witnesses according to criminal procedure, but not immediately with the death penalty, but with the penalty of prison, slavery in the galleys or a beating. Unless, as I have said, he is convicted by clearer proofs, in which case it would be pointless to turn to torture. Therefore what Bodinus observes about the custom in Germany of torturing defendants who plead their innocence even after proof, must be understood to be about simple or civil proof, where the rule holds good that what constitutes grounds in a civil case for conviction is what constitutes grounds in a criminal case for torture.[12] Just as the defendant is also able to uphold his own objection either during the proofs or under torture *mus sie auff der tortur erhalten* [must we again resort to torture], whence it is plainly evident that torture is equivalent to simple proof, so that a person is not usually condemned either on account of the presence of simple proofs, if he sustains his denial under torture, nor on account of their absence if he maintains his assertion under torture. *Landrecht* book 1 article 8 (first part) requires seven witnesses for the penalty of death.[13] Yet nowadays a smaller number is judged to be sufficient, and yet the number must not be considered as much as the evidence of the proofs, which is entrusted to the scrutiny of a judge.

But if this evidence is lacking, then I think it is important for the tranquillity of our conscience that nothing be pronounced about a man's life, and I declare that I will never judge otherwise, unless it is most clearly shown that the contrary is contained in a received law. For the life of a man is a thing of such great value to God that the power over it which we obtain in this life can only be excused by a certain necessity.

But I think that the goal of torture is not so much to obtain a bare confession as to obtain a new light from the circumstances of the confession and, through this opportunity, leading steadily to a calm, lucid and free confession through a spontaneous ratification of a confession made under torture, so that we may judge about his capital punishment with a greater peace of mind.

3. Expiation (1707–1710)[14]

There is a harmony in what the wise man demands, who will not be satisfied with a simple compensation, and will grant what the Roman jurisconsults call a penal action, even when there would be no question of reforming the criminal or of setting an example for others. For when it is known that someone would be incorrigible and that he would be the last of the sinners, it should not be the case that he be left unpunished on that account. This is because a good action must be rewarded, even though he who did it has neither need nor reason to be encouraged, and even though others will not learn of his good fortune and will not be able to benefit from his example. It is true that the reason for punishment is to prevent vice, but that refers to the constitution of punishment, before the sin, but not the execution after the sin. The legislator does not lay down punishments in order to have someone to punish, but in order to show that he wants to prevent sins, but he does not fail to inflict punishments in accordance with his promise to uphold the law when punishments no longer serve to prevent sins. And although the incomparable Grotius, whom I only know through what remains of a part of what he has left, recognizes in this a distinction between the law of God and that of man,[15] because of the sovereign domain of God, I believe that there is nothing to the distinction at all, because God only exercises this domain according to sovereign reason. And when Holy Scripture insinuates that God reserved himself the right of revenge, it is not said in order to destroy the punitive justice of men, but in order to curb the passion for vengeance. It is not about satisfying the passions of the injured party, which are often without limits, but of satisfying the wise, and consequently also the injured party, insofar as they want to listen to reason.

It is as a beautiful piece of music or even well-ordered architecture satisfies well-developed minds. It is most certain that after all the external compensation there also remains the matter of internal compensation to the injured party, which restores his tranquillity of mind, and this is what is neglected too often in the administration of ordinary justice, where one is hardly concerned to remove the source of the feelings of animosity, even though this should be one of the principal duties of judges; but this is not so much their fault as that of the form of our procedures. But it should not be the case that the care of soothing the mind of the injured party goes as far as satisfying everything that an unreasonable passion can claim; and on the other side, even when the injured party would be satisfied with too little, and would not request any punishment, whether by forgetfulness or temperament, reason would demand it for him; it will be the same when the injured party or his family are no longer alive. We should satisfy not only the injured party or his family, but also the public, the wise, and wisdom itself. Aristotle, who was profound in matters of morality, rightly noticed the difference between two kinds of punishment: *kolasis* [punishment] and *timôria* [revenge]; and he observes (*I Rhetoric,* chapter 10) that the first means a punishment done for the good of the one who suffers, and the second means a punishment undertaken in order to satisfy the one who imposes it;[16] and although this distinction does not exactly exhaust the purposes of punishments, it does not fail to clarify what we have just said.

B. Virtue[17]

1. On generosity (1686–1687?)[18]

Generosity, according to the proper meaning of the word, is the virtue that elevates us to perform actions that are worthy of our kind, nature, extraction, or origin, which is heavenly, for as St. Paul says, following a Greek poet whom he himself quotes, we are of the kind or race of God, who is the fountain of minds. It is also in this sense that it is fitting for all men to be generous and to act according to the nobility of human nature, so as not to degenerate or to lower oneself to the level of beasts. This has been touched on very well in the verses of Boethius, Roman senator:

We are all born good and of noble origin,
If we feel in ourselves the divine source.[19]

Thus generosity, which originally meant the virtue of true nobility, is taken generally for virtue, by which we bring ourselves to perform actions that are at the same time elevated and reasonable, for without the lights of reason and justice this elevation is only ambition and vanity.

It must therefore be the case that the truly generous man shows by his actions that he possesses perfections and virtues that are difficult to practice and that are not found in common souls; he will have the courage of Pompey, who when boarding ship for an urgent matter at the risk of being shipwrecked, said to those who wanted to dissuade him: 'it is necessary that I go, but it is not necessary that I live'.[20] He will have the temperance of Alexander, who upon seeing that the wife of Darius, perhaps the most beautiful person in Asia, was in his power, surrendered his passion to his glory.[21] As for justice, this is what he should principally intend in his actions, and of this I will speak later.

The generous man must keep to certain inviolable maxims appropriate for regulating his conduct. Firstly, he must avoid all that is base, and everything that he would not want to be known by everybody. Secondly, when he is in doubt about what he should do, he will take the course that appears to be the most sheltered from any suspicion of sin and injustice. And as much as he must be bold when it comes to risking his commodities and even his life, he must be timid when there is a danger of committing a crime, and it is only in this that he must be timid. Thirdly, he will be suspicious of everything that is easiest and of what the lowest man of the dregs of the race, if he were in his place, would do just as well as him. Fourthly, he will be suspicious of all courses of action and all ways in which self-interest dominates, and it is by a more noble principle that he must act. But since false glory hides itself behind a mask that makes it look like generosity, it must be considered that every action which goes against justice, which is to say against the public good, and in a word everything that is against virtue, is not glorious. Moreover, all actions that will justly be condemned and even punished if they do not succeed, and that chance alone can justify, are never glorious, whatever success they may have. On the contrary, every action that will be praised, even when it is unlucky, is worthy of the one who seeks true glory.

Indeed, we can judge that the good we receive from glory exists only in our mind, for he who cares about glory must always hear of his own fame. From this we can suppose that glory pleases us because it causes us to make a favourable judgement of ourselves through the testimony of others, which increases our satisfaction. But if we know that these people are mistaken, and our racked conscience forces us to inwardly confess our crimes and imperfections, what part could we take in this satisfaction, and what sweetness could we find in these vain appearances, while the inner bitterness which fills our mind is mixed with them? And it is for that reason that we have always regarded the approval of a few excellent men more highly than that of a crowd of the ignorant and vicious.

Above all, we must guard ourselves against actions that appear glorious to corrupt men, but which are in fact detestable because of the evils that they produce in the world; like, for example, unjust and scarcely necessary wars, insurrections, and everything that leads to murder, fire, and public devastation, for all these things can never be excused, unless they serve to avoid greater evils.

Therefore it only remains for us to say something about justice, which is the soul of generosity. It was formerly the profession of the hero to punish the evil and defend the innocent. And what is recognized as unjust will never pass for being generous.

Now the principle of justice is the good of society, or to put it better, the general good, for we are all a part of the universal commonwealth of which God is the monarch, and the great law established in this commonwealth is to procure as much good for the world as we can. This is infallible, supposing that there is a providence that governs all things, even though the mechanisms that it employs are still hidden from our eyes. We must therefore hold as certain that the more a man has done good, or at least endeavoured to do it with all his power (for God, who knows intentions, takes a genuine will for the effect itself) the more he will be happy, and if he has done or even wanted to do great evils, he will receive very great punishments.

In order to know this great maxim one does not need faith, for it suffices to have good sense: for in a complete or perfect body, as is, for example, a plant or an animal, there is a wonderful structure which shows that the author of nature has taken care with it and adjusted it down to the least parts. So by an even greater reason the greatest and most perfect of all bodies, which is the universe, and the noblest parts of the universe, which are souls, will not fail to be well ordered, although this order may still not be apparent to us while we are only able to envisage a part of it. Likewise we see that the pieces or fragments of some crystals of broken rock or of some artificial or natural machine, considered apart and outside of their whole, do not allow us to know the regular shape or the design of the entire body.

We are not therefore born for ourselves, but for the good of society, as are parts for the whole, and we must only consider ourselves as the instruments of God, albeit living and free instruments, able to concur with him according to our choice. If we fail in that we are like monsters and our vices are like diseases in nature, and doubtless we will receive punishment for them in the end so that the order of things is put right, just as we see that diseases weaken and that monsters are more imperfect.

From this we can conclude that the principles of generosity and of justice or piety are merely the same thing, whereas self-interest and self-love, when it is badly regulated, are the principles of cowardice. For generosity, as I said in the beginning, brings us close to the author of our kind or being, that is to say, to God, insofar as we are capable of imitating him. We must therefore act in accordance with the nature of God (who is himself the good of all creatures); we must follow his intention, which orders us to procure the common good, insofar as it depends on us, since charity and justice consist only of this. We must have consideration for the dignity of our nature, the excellence of which consists in the perfection of the mind or in the highest virtue. We must partake in the happiness of those who surround us, as in our own, not seeking our comforts or our interests in what is contrary to the common happiness. Lastly we must consider what the public wants from us and what we ourselves would want if we were put in the place of others, for this is like perceiving the voice of God and the sign of the calling.

But if we scorn these great reasons of the general good, for which we are made, while seeking our own advantages, particularly at the risk of public misery, we would not be generous, whatever profession we may make of following only glory in our actions, and we would not even be happy, whatever success our enterprises may have. For the laws of the universe are inviolable, and we can rest assured that there is no crime that will not receive its punishment in proportion to the evils that it has caused or those which we ought to judge that it could have caused.

2. Letter to Electress Sophie (mid-August (?) 1697)[22]

Madam. I have read only two or three documents of the dispute between the two renowned prelates of France;[23] but even if I had read them all, I would take care not to get involved in judging it. Let us leave this matter to the Pope. For me, I will only give here the ideas that I have had before on this subject, some of which have not been displeasing to Your Electoral Highness. Of all the matters of Theology there are none about which Ladies have more right to judge than this one, because it concerns the nature of love. Although to form a judgement it is not necessary that they possess the great insights of Your Electoral Highness, whose penetration goes almost beyond that of the most profound authors, I would also not want them to be as Mrs Guyon is depicted, that is, ignorant devotees. I would want them to resemble Miss de Scudery, who has clarified the characters and the passions very well in her novels and in her *Conversations about Morals*, or at least like the English Lady Miss Norris, of whom it has been said that she has recently written so well on disinterested love. But let us come to the point.

To love is to find pleasure in the perfections or advantages of others, and especially in their happiness. It is in this way that one loves beautiful things, and especially intelligent substances whose happiness gives us joy and to whom, consequently, we wish only good, since it would give us nothing but pleasure to see them happy. In the same way, those who have the good fortune to know the incomparable virtues of Your Electoral Highness find themselves enlivened.

To love above all things is to find so much pleasure in the perfections and in the happiness of someone that all other pleasures count as nothing, so long as that one remains. From which it follows that, according to reason, what one must love above all things must possess perfections so great that the pleasure they give can efface all other pleasures. And that property can only belong to God.

It is therefore not possible that we could have a love of God above all things separate from our own good, because the pleasure that we find in the contemplation of his perfections is essential to love.

But supposing that beatitude involves pleasures that are not essential to this love, one can love God above all things without being touched by these unfamiliar pleasures.

One can therefore have divine love, even when one believes that one has to be deprived of every other pleasure than the one of this love; and what is more, even when one believes that one has to suffer great pains.

But to suppose that one continues to love God above all things and is nevertheless in eternal torments, is to make a supposition that will never happen.

If someone were to make this supposition, he would be in error, and he would show that he does not sufficiently know the goodness of God, and consequently that he does not yet love him enough.[24]

The Saints who doubtless would have agreed that God will not damn one who loves him above all things, and who have nevertheless said that they would love God even if they would have to be damned, intended to mean, by this false supposition, that the motives of *the love of benevolence* or the virtue of charity are entirely different from the motives of the virtue of hope or the *love of greed* (which does not properly deserve the name of love).

Theologians have always distinguished love arising from benevolence from the kind that arises from concupiscence, as[25] they call it in the idiom of the School; the first is disinterested and, to be precise, only consists in the pleasure which is given by the sight of the perfection and happiness of the object loved, without considering any other good or profit which we can get from it. The second is self-interested, but in a way that can be permitted, and consists, to be precise, in the sight of our own good, without having consideration for the happiness and advantage of others. They relate love of the first kind to the virtue of charity, and love of the second kind to the virtue of hope.

Nevertheless it is true that even the assurance of the other goods that God prepares for those who love him can enter into the motives of a disinterested love, in the sense that it enhances the brilliance of the divine perfections and makes the goodness of God better known. But that is without distinguishing whether he will have this goodness for us or for others. Otherwise, if it were only by a manner of recognition, it would rather be an act of cupidity than of disinterested love: however, nothing prevents the actions of these two virtues, of charity and hope, being exercised jointly.

There is, moreover, a great reflection of one of these two virtues upon the other. For when we are not satisfied with our present love, and we ask from God a greater knowledge in order to have more love, we carry out an act of hope, in as much as our own good is the motive for it. But it is an act of benevolence inasmuch as the pleasure that we experience in seeing that God is so perfect makes us wish that he be better known by his creatures, in order to be better loved by them and so that his glory is more conspicuous, without, preferably, letting the motive of our own good become involved.

It is true that one could not give any good to God, but nevertheless the benevolence that one offers to him makes us act as if it could be possible. One of the strongest indications of a love of God which is sincere and disinterested is being satisfied with what he has already done, in the assurance that it is always the best: but also trying to make what remains to be done as good and in keeping with his presumptive will as is possible for us. In order to love him, we must commend his certain will which is apparent from the past, and try to satisfy his presumptive will with regard to the future: for although the Kingdom of God comes just as well without us, nevertheless our good intention and ardent will to do good is what makes us share in it the most. And without that there is no benevolence in us.

I wanted to go further into this matter some years ago, before it became stirred up in France. And it was some time before that that I talked about it in the preface of a book on law, where, recognizing that charity is of course the foundation of justice, I talked about it in such a way, and gave the following definitions:

Justice is charity conforming to wisdom.

Wisdom is the science of happiness.

Charity is a universal benevolence.

Benevolence is a habit of loving.

To love is to find pleasure in the good, perfection, and happiness of others.

And by this definition one can resolve (I added) a great difficulty, important even in Theology, of how it is possible that there be a non-mercenary love, detached from hope and from fear, as well as from all concern for self-interest.

The fact is that the happiness or the perfection of others, in giving us pleasure, immediately forms part of our own happiness.

For everything that pleases is desired for itself, and not through interest.

It is a good in itself, and not a useful good.

It is thus that the contemplation of beautiful things is agreeable in itself, and that a painting by Raphael affects him who looks at it with enlightened eyes, although he derives no profit from it.

And when the object, the perfection of which pleases us, is itself capable of happiness, then the affection that one has for it becomes that which properly deserves to be called love.

However, all loves are surpassed by the one which has God for an object, and only God can be loved with reason above all things.

For nothing could be more successfully loved, because there is nothing happier, and nothing which more deserves to be so.

Also, there is nothing more beautiful and more capable of giving pleasure and satisfaction to those who love him and who take pleasure in his happiness.

And the more his wisdom and his power are raised to the highest degree, they do not form part of our happiness merely as a part forms part of the whole, or as other pleasures or loves form part of it, but they constitute the whole of our true happiness.

This is the sense of what I had published in Latin in 1693.[26] But I have been formulating these ideas since my youth.

3. Definitions (1701–1705?)[27]

Justice is a constant will to act so that nobody has reason to complain about us.

To complain about someone is to blame him for the fact that he causes us harm. By *harm,* I also understand the diminution of, or the impediment to our good.

To blame someone is to claim that he acts in an unreasonable manner.

A voluntary action of a person is *unreasonable*[28] when the appearances are that it tends against his own good.

The *good for someone* is that which contributes to his happiness, and the evil is the contrary of this.

Happiness is the state of lasting joy.

Joy consists in the sensing of perfections.

4. The true piety (before 1710?)[29]

I must ultimately not spare myself from saying that this discourse will be able to contribute to giving a *better idea of the true piety* than is often found among many of those who parade it in order to insult others, and condemn all those who are not attached to the formalities that please them. I do not speak of those who are hypocrites absolutely, and who secretly make fun of everything that they revere in public; but of those who deceive themselves and applaud from the depths of their soul their deeds and thoughts, as if they were special friends of the divinity, while they dishonour it with the bad qualities which they attribute to God and, by their own maliciousness, would want to authorize by his example. And if their error was innocent, there would perhaps be no need to disabuse them, but this so-called piety is a source of impious actions and causes an infinity of evils. And those who do not have piety have some resemblance to the pagans who found in their Gods all that was necessary to authorize their crimes. Apart from the fact that from this false devotion it is only one step to hypocrisy, a little reflection is capable of opening their eyes and of making them understand that they are only honouring a phantom of God; and having no good principles, they will have nothing to put in place of the errors from which they will be freed.

The good principles that make piety sound, which is to say true and lasting at the same time, will be in part implied in the work that one does in public. We must recognize in God a *power* and an infinite *goodness;* these are the perfections of which the first should oblige us to be good, and the second should make us want to be so. But both would not suffice if they were not supported in God by an immense *wisdom*, which makes him choose and effectuate the true and even the greatest good.

Some people will say that they recognize all that, but they must be careful that their consequences and practices do not belie them, for practice is the touchstone of faith. And it is not only what people themselves practice, but what they do to apply it to God, that betrays them.

They depict him as limited in his views, disordering and repairing at any time his own work, attached to trifling matters, formal, capricious, without pity towards some and without justice towards others, gratifying without subject, punishing without measure, indifferent to virtue, showing his greatness through evil, impotent with regard to the good, or only half-wanting it; making use of an arbitrary power, and using it at the wrong moment, lastly feeble, unreasonable, cunning, and in a word such as they show themselves to be when they have power or when they think they have it: for they imitate only too well the idol that they worship.

It is not only those who are strict in matters of dogma who think and act so poorly, but there are many people everywhere who speak of the goodness of God while they destroy the idea, and only conserve the name of it. There is no mark of true piety more beautiful or more certain than what is given in Holy Scripture, that one cannot love God, who is invisible, when one does not love his fellow man, who is visible. Those who never trouble themselves with the truth, with instruction, those who have a hard soul, who reduce justice to harshness, and who never conceive that one could not be just without being charitable because one is only the administrator of goods that God has entrusted to us in order to give delight to others; those who enjoy mudslinging and reckless judgements, who attempt to give ridicule to others while flattering their own vanity as if they were high above them; lastly not only those who look for their profit, their pleasure and their glory in the misfortune of others, but also those who are never passionate about procuring the common good and about taking the misery from those who are within their reach, and generally those that show themselves to be without wisdom and without charity – they boast in vain of a piety that they hardly know, whatever expression they make.

C. Pleasure and Happiness

1. On the happy life (spring–autumn 1676)[30]

Down here, the happy life consists in a soul which is completely content and peaceful. In order to achieve this, we must observe the following points.

(1) We should make use of reason as much as is possible in order to know goods and evils, and in order to distinguish the great from the small, and the false from the true; in order to decide what should be done and not done in the course of this life. In a word, it is necessary to understand what reason commands, and from that comes *wisdom*.

(2) We should have a firm intention to execute the commandments of reason, without any distress or passion being able to divert us from such a noble plan. In a word, we have to try to follow in practice exactly what right reason has taught us in theory, and from that comes this habit which we call *virtue*.

(3) Finally, having done our utmost to know the true goods, and to attain them, we have to be content, whatever happens, and we must be convinced that everything that is outside of our power, that is to say, everything that we have not been able to obtain after having done our duty, is not numbered among the true goods. And consequently, in a word, we should always have our mind at rest, without complaining about anything. And this state of mind is what produces *happiness* or tranquillity of the soul.

Since those three points are important and cover a lot of ground, it will be appropriate to explain them distinctly, one at a time. But the words will be useless if the one who reads them does not give them all the attention of which he is capable, and if he does not reflect, at every word, on what he has done so far and on what he must do in the future. That is the true way to benefit from them. For if he thinks he is able to read this as a passing discourse made to please rather than to instruct, it would be better not to go further in the reading which will only serve to make him more guilty.

2. Happiness (1694–1698)[31]

3[32] *Happiness* is a lasting state of pleasure. Thus it is good to abandon or moderate some pleasures which can be harmful by causing pains or by preventing better and more lasting pleasures.

2 *Wisdom* is the science of happiness, and is what must be studied above everything else.

1 *Virtue* is the habit of acting in accordance with wisdom. Practice should accompany knowledge.

4 *Pleasure* is a knowledge or feeling of perfection not only in us, but also in others, because that then excites some pleasure in us.

5 To love is to find pleasure in the perfection of others.[33]

6 Justice is charity or a habit of loving in accordance with wisdom. Thus when one is inclined to justice, one tries to procure good for everyone, insofar as one reasonably can, but in proportion to the needs and merits of each person; and even if one is also sometimes obliged to punish the wicked, it is for the general good.

Now we must explain the feeling or the knowledge of perfection. The confused perception of some perfection constitutes the pleasure of the senses, but this pleasure can be mixed with greater imperfections which arise from it, just as a fruit of pleasing taste and nice smell can conceal a poison. This is why one must resist the pleasures of the senses, just as one distrusts a stranger, or rather a flattering enemy.

7 There are two kinds of knowledge, that of facts, and that of reasons. That of facts is perception, that of reasons is intelligence.[34]

8 Knowledge of reasons perfects us because it teaches us of universal and eternal truths, which express the perfect being. However knowledge of facts is like that of the streets of a town, which is useful to us while we remain there, after which we do not want to weigh the memory down with it.[35]

8[36] The pleasures of sense that most approach the pleasures of the mind, and are the purest and most certain, are those of music and symmetry, one being the pleasure of the ears, the other being pleasure of the eyes, for it is easy to understand the reasons of the harmony or of that perfection which gives us pleasure. The only thing to be feared from this is of making use of it too often.

9 We must not distrust the pleasures that arise from intelligence or reasons, when we penetrate the reason of the reason of perfections, that is to say, when we see them follow from their source, which is the absolutely perfect being.

10 The perfect being is called God. He is the final reason of things, and the cause of causes. Being the sovereign wisdom and sovereign power, he has always chosen the best and always acts in an orderly way.

11 We are happy when we love God, and God, who has done everything perfectly, could not fail to arrange everything thus, to elevate creatures to the perfection of which they are capable through the union with him, which can only consist in the mind.

12 However we could not love God without knowing his perfections or his beauty. And as we would only know him through his emanations, there are two ways of seeing his beauty, namely in the knowledge of eternal truths,[37] explaining the reasons in themselves, and in the knowledge of the harmony of the universe, by applying reasons to facts. That is to say, we must know the wonders of reason and the wonders of nature.

13 The wonders of reason and of eternal truths that our mind discovers in itself in the sciences of reasoning are about numbers, shapes, good or evil, justice and injustice.

14 The wonders of corporeal nature are the system of the universe, the structure of the bodies of animals, the causes of the rainbow, of the magnet, of tidal ebb and flow, and a thousand other similar things.

15 We must hold for certain that the more a mind desires to know the order, the reason, the beauty of things that God has produced, and the more it is moved to imitate this order in the things that God has left to its management, the more it will be happy.

16 Consequently it is very true that one could not love God without loving his own brother, that one could not have wisdom without having charity, which is the touchstone of true virtue, and even that one advances his own good while procuring that of others, because it is an eternal law of the reason and harmony of things that the works of each person will

follow it.[38] Thus the sovereign wisdom has ordered all things so well that our duty must also give rise to our happiness, that every virtue produces its reward, and that every crime is punished sooner or later.

VIRTUE *is the habit of acting in accordance with wisdom*, because practice must accompany knowledge, in order that the exercise of good actions becomes easy and natural for us, and passes into habit, because custom is another nature.

WISDOM *is the science of happiness*. This is what one must study more than any other science, because nothing is more desirable than happiness. This is why we must endeavour to ensure that our mind is always above the subject matter with which it is occupied, so that it often makes reflections on the end or goal of what it does by saying to itself from time to time: 'what am I doing?', 'to what good is that?', 'let us come to the important point'. Thus one must be careful not to become distracted by trifling matters, or with what becomes a trifling matter when one is too taken with it.

HAPPINESS *is a lasting state of joy*.[39] This is why our joy and our pleasure should not have harmful consequences that cause a much greater or longer lasting sadness or pain.[40] It is in this choice of joys and pleasures and in the means of obtaining them or avoiding sadness that consists the science of happiness. Some pleasures[41] cause much greater or longer-lasting pains, or prevent greater and more enduring pleasures. And there are pains or difficulties that are extremely useful and instructive. Thus it is in their choice, or in the means of obtaining or avoiding them, that consists the science of happiness.

JOY *is the total pleasure that results from everything the soul feels at once*. This is why one can have joy in the midst of great pains, when the pleasures that one feels at the same time are sufficiently great and capable of blotting the pains out: just like in the case of that Spanish slave who, having killed a Carthaginian murderer of his master, was beside himself with joy, and made light of the torments that the torturers were able to invent.[42]

PLEASURE *is the feeling of some perfection*, and this perfection that causes pleasure can be found not only in us, but also elsewhere. For when we notice it, this very knowledge excites some perfection in us, because the representation of the perfection is also a perfection. This is why it is good to familiarize oneself with objects that have many perfections. And we must avoid the hate and envy which prevent us from taking pleasure in these objects.

TO LOVE *is to find pleasure in the happiness of others.*[43] Thus *the habit of loving someone is nothing other than* BENEVOLENCE by which we want the good of others, not for the profit that we gain from it, but because it is agreeable to us in itself.

CHARITY *is a general benevolence.* And JUSTICE *is charity in accordance with wisdom.* Thus when one is in the mood to want and to make everyone happy, as much as it depends on us, one has charity; and when charity is well ruled by wisdom, so that nobody can complain about it, there stems from it the virtue which is called justice, so that one does not do harm to someone without necessity, and that one does good as much as one can, but especially where it is best employed.[44]

There are two kinds of knowledge, that of facts, which is called PERCEPTION, *and that of reasons, which is called* INTELLIGENCE. Perception is of singular things, intelligence has for its object the universals or the eternal truths, and it is for this reason that knowledge of reasons perfects us forever, and makes us return everything to the final reason of things, that is to God, who is the source of happiness. However, knowledge of facts is as that of the streets of a town, which is useful to us while we remain there, after which we do not want to weigh the memory down with it. Thus the pleasure from knowing reasons is much more worthy than that from learning facts. And the facts that are most important to consider are those that concern things that can contribute the most to making us have the free spirit to reason justly and to act according to reason. Such are the facts the knowledge of which is useful for the order that we must have in life, and in the usage of time; for the exercise of virtue; for the care of health, because diseases prevent us from acting and thinking; for the art of living with other men, because of all external things what is of most use to man is man, all men having the same true interest. Therefore we must make the most of their assistance for obtaining knowledge of the truth, seeking out the virtuous and the wise, and being able to associate with other men if need be, without receiving any harm from them.

3. A dialogue (after 1695?)[45]

CHARINUS:[46] I have wanted to talk with you for a long time, and so you have not been the least reason for my journey from far away. I have read the majority of your published works, in which it is as if I have seen a kind of dawn rising, heralding a new light. But I have not sufficiently understood many things, and there are many ideas that you have put forward that I hope you will not allow to perish. The urge has come several times to approach you through letters, but I was deterred by the fear of the prolixity necessary between people who are far apart, who are seldom unable to express themselves face to face in a few words, and I was unwilling to put pressure on you privately when you do so much in public. Therefore I put it off until such time as I might be able to address your great wisdom in person. But now my prayer will be granted when I prevail upon your kindness, known everywhere, and get you to teach a man who is eager to learn, to dispel ambiguity and to correct my mistakes; finally if the good mind of Charinus seems to you worthy of this honour, you may receive a devout supporter of the truth into that sublime sanctuary of your serene mind, from which you may look down on others and see them all astray, wandering in search of the way of truth.[47]

THEOPHILUS: I am glad to be dealing with a man who has shown himself desirous of the truth with great arguments. But the acquaintance with the truth, whose diffusion is immense in itself, ought to be directed to the enjoyment of the good, lest the human mind should wander in vain amid useless curiosity. Moreover, all men seek the good, but the true goods are procured by only a few. The majority do not think of the greatest of things except in passing, and soon they are thrown back towards common pursuits by the tides of the affections; they do not dwell easily with themselves, nor do they dwell with God. Therefore they lead the wandering life (as you say) as if by chance, and they do not find the way to happiness, nor do they even search for it. *Wisdom* is to me nothing other than the science of happiness. I regard *happiness* as a state of enduring joy, and *joy* as a great predominance of what is pleasing, so that either no inconveniences are present, or they are of little consequence to the pleasure of the moment.[48] For the pleasant and the unpleasant consist of particular perceptions, and we are able at the same time to be affected both by pleasure and pain through the variety of the senses and of objects; but from the conjunction of all present perceptions and from what I call the whole complex of feeling there results what we call joy and sadness, by the great excess of either the pleasant or the unpleasant, in which the attention is drawn away from the opposite feeling. However, *pleasantness* lies in the feeling of perfection, and this feeling is no doubt involved in every pleasure, but pleasures whose reason is not sufficiently understood, such as those that are perceived by the external senses, can conceal greater evils in the future, like a pleasant-tasting poison. Therefore we must strive for those clear and pure pleasures, whose perfection lies not only in the sense, but also in the intellect, and these we call the pleasures of the mind, in which it is clear that evils cannot lie hidden. These pleasures eventually arise safe and sound, and are able to bring forth enduring joy; through these pleasures there is a direct road to happiness.

CHARINUS: If only we had definitions for all concepts like the ones you have given for wisdom, happiness, joy, and pleasantness! And truly you show most beautifully what goal we should set ourselves; you also show the way by which it can in some measure be approached; and you include whatever teaching is to be had from a few ancient philosophers, in order that we may be unhappy as little as possible. But I fear that your definitions themselves show that happiness is outside of our power. For who among mortals would promise to himself enduring joy and constant excesses of the pleasant over the unpleasant? How many changes there are in the fortunes of men, how often men are vexed by men, and even if you assume that savage enemies can be appeased by wile to some extent, how often we experience nature herself as unfriendly, indeed deaf and inexorable! How many men are seized by public misfortune, swallowed by waters, or crushed by earthquake, not to mention the seeds of perpetual sickness received from birth and external attacks and other sources of personal evils! What use is the knowledge of happiness to those who are deprived of the means of obtaining it? It is as if the most skilled expert in military knowledge did not have a soldier whom he could lead.

THEOPHILUS: If all our life, which we pass in this arena, were contained in a brief space of years, there could be no reply to your observation. Yet you rightly acknowledge that the teachings I proscribed would not be useless even if our whole life were limited to but a few years. For at least we shall come as close to happiness as will be allowed, and when we are acquainted with the sources of joy, the greatest part of which is within us, we shall draw from them as much joy as will be permitted to be set against chance evils. And since every joy or sadness depends on the attention of the soul, I hold that man is able to be equipped with the technique for attaining joy as a result of its practice in even the hardest circumstances, and thus is able to discover within himself the pleasures of the soul, to which all pains of the body yield. That was the opinion of the ancients, and a great author of our time has agreed with it.[49] And reason is strengthened by examples, for, to pass over the martyrs to religious faith, and not appeal to the ancient gymnosophists, the present barbarians in America are not helped by teaching, but only by the vigour of the soul, yet they mock those who burn them, and they triumph over the cruelty of their enemies, armed with the desire for glory or rather with the fear of disgrace, lest they seem to have degenerated from the virtue of their parents. What is lacking in our innate strength will have to be supplied by art, education and use, and I would wish that they be given whatever means were permitted to ascend this peak of strength; but such harshness of evils, which would force us men to have recourse to a remedy so noble, is rare.

Notes

1 G III 386–9. Latin.

2 Hugo Grotius, *On the Law of War and Peace,* 1.1.4.

3 Ibid.

4 Xenophon, *The Education of Cyrus,* 1.3.17.

5 VE 11–13. Latin.

6 Leibniz actually wrote 'guilty' here, though that is clearly a slip for 'innocent'.

7 'One witness is not enough to convict a man accused of any crime or offence he may have committed. A matter must be established by the testimony of two or three witnesses.'

8 *Constitutio criminalis Carolina* (1532).

9 'It is further to be noticed that no one shall be definitely sentenced to penal sanction on the basis of any indication of a suspicious sign or upon suspicion, rather on that basis there may only be examination under torture; when the indications are sufficient (as will be found below), then the person shall be finally condemned to penal sanction; however, that must take place upon the basis of his own confession or a witness proof procedure (as will be found plainly elsewhere in this ordinance), and not on the basis of presumption or indication.' *Carolina,* art. 22, from John H. Langbein (1974), *Prosecuting Crime in the Renaissance,* Cambridge, Massachusetts: Harvard University Press, p. 273.

10 'When a crime is proved with at least two or three credible good witnesses, who testify from a true knowledge, then there shall be process and judgement of penal law according to the nature of the case.' *Carolina,* art. 67, from Langbein, op. cit., p. 284.

11 'When the accused still will not confess after sufficient proof, it shall be

declared to him that the crime is proven of him, in order that his confession can be secured that much easier; and when, notwithstanding, he persists in not confessing, although (as above) it has been sufficiently proved of him, then he shall nonetheless be condemned on account of the proven crime without any examination under torture.' *Carolina*, art. 69, from Langbein, op. cit., p. 285.

12 Heinrich von Bode (Henricus Bodinus), *Disputatio juridica de abusu et usu torturae* (10 July 1697).

13 The Landrecht was the first part of the *Sachsenspiegel* [Saxon Mirror] compiled in 1221–4 by Eike von Repgow. The Landrecht concerned criminal and civil law. The second part, the Lehnrecht, concerned feudal regulations.

14 Gr 880–2. French.

15 Grotius, op. cit., 2.20.4.

16 'Punishment is inflicted for the sake of the person punished; revenge for that of the punisher, to satisfy his feelings', ACW 1369b13–15.

17 See also VI.B.1.

18 A VI iv 2718–23. French.

19 Boethius, *On the consolation of philosophy*, III.6.

20 Plutarch, *Life of Pompey*, 50.2.

21 Plutarch, *Life of Alexander*, 21.7.

22 A I xiv 54–9. French.

23 Fénelon and Bossuet. Leibniz is referring to their debate over whether one can have a truly disinterested love for God.

24 In a draft copy of this letter the sentence originally continued: 'although he nevertheless could love him above all things through other motives'. Leibniz then added, and deleted, the following: 'But it is possible to love God above all things at the present time even if one were to believe that one must stop loving him, and that one must be damned eternally. For the change that can happen in me does not prevent me finding pleasure now in what is lovable. And even if I were to find that his perfections lead him to damn me one day because of what I will be then, will they be less great and less lovable?'

25 Reading *comme* for *come*.

26 'Preface to the *Diplomatic Code of People's Rights*' (1693), pp. 149–52 of this volume.

27 Gr 666–7. French.

28 Here Leibniz originally wrote: 'when it is against the good of the one who acts, and when he could easily judge that it is apparently contrary to his good'.

29 Gr 499–500. French.

30 A VI iii 668–9. French.

31 Gr 579–84. French.

32 The numbering is Leibniz's own, and according to Grua indicates a change of plan.

33 Here Leibniz originally wrote: '5 Our internal perfections are science, knowledge and vigour.'

34 Here Leibniz originally wrote: '7 Knowledge of facts helps us, but knowledge of reasons perfects us.'

35 Here Leibniz originally wrote: '8 The pleasure of the mind consists in the knowledge of perfections by their reasons, which is to say it consists in the knowledge of the perfect being, who is the final reason of things and of their emanations.'

36 Sic.

37 Here Leibniz originally added: 'which consist in reasons, numbers, shapes, orders, changes'.

38 Here Leibniz originally wrote: 'The touchstone of true piety is the desire to procure good. One does not have it when one does not have an ardent desire.'

39 Here Leibniz originally wrote: 'But some pleasures, especially the most sensual, afterwards cause much greater and longer-lasting pains, or prevent greater and longer-lasting pleasures.' After deleting that, he then wrote and deleted the following: 'We must distinguish between joy and pleasure: we can have joy in the midst of pains; we must also consider that joy is always accompanied by contentment, but that says something more.'

40 Among Leibniz's many changes to this sentence was the deletion of this: 'It is in this choice of joys and pleasures, and in the means to obtain them or avoid sadness, that consists the science of happiness.'

41 Here Leibniz originally wrote: 'especially the most sensual'.

42 An example drawn from Livy's *The History of Rome*, 21.2. Leibniz also mentions it in the *Theodicy* §255.

43 Here Leibniz originally added: 'Thus it is nothing other than a benevolence which is disinterested.'

44 Here Leibniz originally added: 'The best way of feeling perfection is the knowledge of perfections by their reasons.'

45 Gr 588–90. Latin.

46 The names of the characters are borrowed from *Pacidius Philalethi*, a dialogue on continuity and motion written in October/November 1676 (LC 129–221).

47 An adaptation of Lucretius *On the nature of things*, II.9–10: 'from which you may look down on others and see them all astray, wandering in search of the path of life'.

48 Here Leibniz originally wrote: 'However the pleasant consists of a feeling of perfection. For pleasure is something particular.'

49 Descartes. See his letter to Princess Elizabeth, 6 October 1645, in John Cottingham, Robert Stoothoff, Dugald Murdoch and Anthony Kenny (eds), *The Philosophical Works of Descartes Vol. III*, Cambridge: Cambridge University Press, 1991, p. 272.

VI. THEOLOGY

A. The Existence of God[1]

1. On the reality of truth (August 1677)[2]

It is true, or rather it is necessary, that a circle is the most capacious of isoperimetric shapes, even if no circle really exists. Likewise if neither I nor you nor anyone else of us exists.

Likewise even if none of those things exist which are contingent, or in which no necessity is understood, such as is the visible world and other similar things.

Therefore because this truth does not depend on our thinking, it is necessary that there is something real in it.

And because that truth is eternal or necessary, this reality that is in it independent of our thinking will also exist from eternity.

This reality is a certain existence in actuality. For this actual truth always subsists in actuality objectively.

Therefore a necessary being exists, or one from whose essence there is existence.

To put it more briefly: the truth of necessary propositions is eternal. Truth is a certain reality independent of our thinking. Certainly some eternal reality always exists. That is, the truth of necessary propositions always exists. Therefore some necessary being exists.

Whatever exists is possible. Some necessary being exists. Therefore some necessary being is possible.

The minor is proved thus: whatever in actuality is objective, that exists. A certain necessary thing is in actuality objective. Therefore a certain necessary thing exists.

I prove the minor again: the truth of necessary propositions is in actuality objective. The truth of necessary propositions is necessary. Therefore a certain necessary thing is in actuality objective.

From this it is evident that there are as many necessary things as there are necessary truths. These necessities can be combined, any one to any one, because any two propositions can be connected to prove a new one, when the means of joining them have been added.

(A difficulty is that the same proposition can be demonstrated in many ways. Yet there are not many causes of the same thing.)

Therefore all realities existing in eternal truths, with no one thinking about them, will have some real connection to each other.

Truths arise from natures or essences. Therefore even essences or natures are certain realities, always existing.

The same nature comes together to form innumerable others, and is able to come together with any other.

Those realities that are in natures in reality, or as they say objectively,[3] are not distinguished by time and place. Because they combine.

The objective realities of conceivable natures and of truths are likewise the same in many other respects.

Those realities are not substances.

A substance existing by necessity is unlimited, i.e. it contains all realities in itself.

Plato, dialogue 10 of the *Laws* – the soul is what moves itself.[4]

2. On necessary or eternal truths (August 1677)[5]

Because, with other things removed, there would remain the truth or possibility of propositions (which, it is clear and can be shown about every one, exist without the existence of subjects), it is for this reason impossible that nothing exists. And this is now evident from a different source, from the fact that something exists. Therefore a cause is necessarily present. There are as many possibilities or truths as there are propositions. But all things seem to exist in one being, which contains ideas. This proof of a necessary and ideal being is not to be disregarded.

As many conclude the same thing in different languages, names are not in the cause but in the nature of things themselves. If no one thought, the impossibility of a square larger than an isoperimetric circle would still exist. And since it is only a mode, it is necessary that its subject be something. Necessary truths follow from natures. Therefore natures are eternal too, not just truths. A plurality of truths joined with each other produce new truths. And there is no truth which does not produce a new truth when united with any other truth. Therefore anything in any truth that exists objectively from eternity is united with any other truth. And this is much more obvious from the fact that one nature joins in constituting another nature. Natures and truths are modes. The reason why a necessary proposition is true when no one is thinking must be objectively in some subject. The cause why the aforesaid proposition about the circle and the square is true is not in the nature of the circle alone nor in the nature of the square alone, but also in other natures that enter into it – for instance, of the equal and of the perimeter. The proximate cause of one thing is singular. And its cause must be in something. Therefore it must be in that in which is found the nature of the circle, the square, and the other things; that is, in the subject of ideas, or God.

3. A proof of the existence of God from his essence (January 1678)[6]

(1) The possible existence or possibility of any thing, and the essence of that same thing, are inseparable (that is, if one of them exists in the region of ideas or of truths, or of realities, the other also exists in it. That is, given the truth of the existence of one, the truth of the other exists, for truths exist even if the things do not exist and are not thought to exist by anyone . . .)

Therefore assuming that

(2) The possible existence or possibility of God, and the essence of God, are inseparable (for the essence of a thing is the specific reason of its possibility).

Now, however

(3) The essence of God and his actual existence are inseparable.[7] See the proof of this under 'NB' and 'NB NB'.

Therefore it must be concluded

(4) The possible existence or possibility of God, and his actual existence, are inseparable.

Or, which is the same thing

(5) Assuming God is possible, it follows that God actually exists.

The third proposition is proved in this way:

(3) The essence of God and his actual existence are inseparable.

NB

I prove it firstly, for

((1)) The essence of God and the greatest perfection are inseparable (*ex hypothesi*, for we suppose the essence of God contains the greatest perfection).

((2)) The greatest perfection, and every perfection in kind are inseparable

((3)) Actual existence is a perfection in kind.

Therefore

The essence of God and his actual existence are inseparable.

But since this argument can still be tightened into an abbreviated form, and the mention of perfection can be removed, I therefore prove it, secondly, in this way:

NB NB

((4)) The essence of God includes necessity of existence (for by the name of God we understand some necessary being).

((5)) One whose essence includes necessity of existence, has an essence that is inseparable from existence (for otherwise any given thing is only possible or contingent).

Therefore

The essence and existence of God are inseparable.

Therefore we have finally concluded

If God is possible, he actually exists, and now all that needs to be proved is that a most perfect being, or at least a necessary being, is possible.

Comments

(1) This argument has found it very hard to get assent among men, because it is without an example, which is not surprising since only the essence of God has this privilege that its existence can be deduced from itself *a priori* without supposing any actuality or experience, because God is also the first being, either being from itself or a being from whose essence existence follows. But he who does not reflect on this, even if he may feel himself to be convinced, and even if he does not have anything solid to say to this argument, he will nevertheless always suspect some deception in it, and will scarcely be able to trust himself and his own argument; just as tends to happen in all paradoxical conclusions.

(2) Cartesians work with conceptions or ideas alone, but they do not adequately bring out the force of this argument, as I have learned from experience, when they have compared their argument with mine. That is why they have not noticed that they are only able to conclude that God

exists by supposing his possibility. For they believe that from the latter argument it is proved absolutely that God exists, which is false.

(3) Essences, truths, or objective realities of concepts do not depend either on the existence of subjects or on our thinking, but even if no one thinks about them and no examples of them existed, nevertheless in the region of ideas or truths, as I would say, i.e. objectively, it would remain true that these possibilities or essences actually exist, as do the eternal truths resulting from them.

(4) Eternal truths are not to be considered in this argument as hypotheticals assuming actual existence, for otherwise we would have a circular argument. That is, from the assumed existence of God his existence would be proved. Of course in saying that the essence of God involves existence, it must not be understood to mean that if God exists he necessarily exists, but in this way: objectively, with no one thinking about it, it is unconditionally, absolutely and purely true that the essence and existence of God are inseparably connected in that region of essences or ideas.

(5) As in the region of eternal truths, or in the realm of ideas that exists objectively, there subsist unity, the circle, power, equality, heat, the rose, and other realities or forms or perfections, even if no individual beings exist, and these universals were not thought about; so also there is found, among other forms or objective realities, actual existence, not as is found in the world or in examples, but as some kind of universal form, which, if it is inseparably connected with some other essence or form in the realm of ideas, results in a being necessarily existing in fact.

(6) In order that a possible objection against our argument may be easily removed, we should consider that all those who grant that God is a necessary being must also grant that some argument similar to ours can be made about God. For one is necessary, or being from itself, whose existence necessarily follows from his essence, or is inseparable from it, therefore there must be some such argument through which we can conclude the actual existence of God from consideration of his essence or possible existence alone, such that anyone who perfectly considered the essence of God would clearly see *a priori* that necessary existence follows from it. Therefore all the objections that are usually raised against our argument at first glance (namely that actualities cannot be deduced from possibilities, and others of that kind) immediately fail, for the same objections can also be made to the former argument through which anyone who considers the matter would understand that existence follows from the essence of God (as I have shown). Therefore it is evident from this

that anyone who wants to attack our superior argument must make some specific objection against it, which may not even be an objection to the latter argument. But since our superior argument is not concerned with particulars, the only objection that can therefore be made against it is this – it may be denied that the concept of God, either as the most perfect being or a necessary being, is possible. For this point alone could not be an objection to the person who specifically considered the essence of God, and who noticed that existence followed from it, since every essence which we perceive distinctly does not imply a contradiction, but is possible. Therefore this alone remains to be done to demonstrate the existence of God, that his possibility, i.e. of the most perfect being or at least necessary being, is demonstrated. For either it is to be said that the necessary being is an impossible fiction, or it is to be admitted that anyone who understands its specific nature (whatsoever it may ultimately be) will also understand, from the essence alone, i.e. *a priori*, that it has within it necessity of existence, or the inseparability of essence and existence.

(7) Spinoza reasons thus, following Descartes: it is the same to say that something is contained in the nature or concept of some thing, as to say that that very something is true about that thing (just as it is contained in the concept of a triangle, or follows from its essence, that its three angles are equal to two right angles). But necessary existence is contained in the concept of God in the same way. Therefore it is true to say about God that necessary existence is in him, or that he exists. To this argument, and others like it, it can be objected that all those propositions are conditional, for to say that three angles equal to two right angles are involved in the nature or concept of a triangle is to say only that if a triangle should exist, then it would have this property. So in the same way, even if it be granted that necessary existence is part of the concept of God, still the only thing that will be inferred from that is that if God exists, then he will have this property (of necessary existence), or that if God exists, he exists necessarily. Our argument, however, does not suffer from this difficulty, but proves something more, namely that if God is merely possible, he necessarily exists in fact.

If a necessarily existing being is possible, it will certainly exist, for if a necessarily existing being does not exist it will be impossible because it implies a contradiction that some being exists necessarily and yet does not exist. Therefore the issue comes down to this, that we show that a necessary being, or an essence from which existence follows, is possible.

4. Extract from a letter concerning the Cartesian demonstration for the existence of God, sent to the editor of the *Journal de Trévoux* (end of June 1701)[8]

I have already explained elsewhere my opinion on the demonstration of the existence of God given by St. Anselm and revived by Descartes, the substance of which is that that which contains in its idea all the perfections, or is the greatest of all possible beings, also includes existence in its essence, since existence is among the perfections, and that otherwise something could be added to what is perfect. I hold the middle ground between those who take this reasoning to be a sophism, and the opinion of Reverend Father Lamy, explained here, who takes it to be a complete demonstration. I therefore grant that it is a demonstration, but an imperfect one, which requires us to suppose as a truth something which also deserves to be demonstrated. For it is tacitly supposed that God, or rather the perfect being, is possible. If this point were also demonstrated properly, then it could be said that the existence of God would be demonstrated geometrically, *a priori*. And this shows what I have already said, that we cannot reason perfectly about ideas without knowing their possibility: geometers have paid attention to this, but the Cartesians not enough. Nevertheless it can be said that this demonstration does not cease to be considerable, and presumptive, so to speak; for every being must be held possible until its impossibility is proved. However I doubt that Reverend Father Lamy had grounds to say that the demonstration was adopted by the School, since the author of the marginal notes rightly remarks that St. Thomas rejected it.

Be that as it may, an even simpler demonstration could be formed by not mentioning the perfections at all, so as not to be stopped by those who would take it upon themselves to deny that all perfections are compatible, and consequently that the idea in question is possible. For in simply saying that God is a Being from itself or primitive *Ens a se* [Being from itself], that is to say, a being that exists from its essence, it is easy to conclude from this definition that such a being, if it is possible, exists, or rather that this conclusion is a corollary which is immediately derived from the definition and hardly differs from it at all. For as the essence of the thing is only that which makes its possibility in particular, it is quite clear that for a thing to exist by its essence is for it to exist by its possibility. And if *the Being from itself* were defined in even closer terms, by saying that it is *the being which must exist because it is possible*, it is clear that the only thing that could be said against the existence of such a being would be to deny its possibility.

We could also offer to this subject a modal proposition which would be one of the best fruits of all logic, namely that *if the necessary being is possible, it exists*. For *the necessary being* and the *being by its essence* are nothing but the same thing. Thus the argument taken from this angle appears to have some solidity, and those who claim that actual existence can never be inferred from notions, ideas, definitions, or possible essences alone, in fact fall back into what I have just said, that is to say that they deny the possibility of the Being from itself. But it is right to note that this very approach serves to show that they are wrong, and ultimately fills the gap in the demonstration. For if the *Being from itself* is impossible, all the beings by others are also impossible, because they exist, ultimately, only through the *Being from itself*; and therefore nothing could exist. This reasoning leads us to another important modal proposition, equal to the preceding one, and which together with it completes the demonstration. It can be expressed like this: *if the necessary being does not exist, there is no possible being*. It seems that this demonstration had not been taken so far until now; however I have also endeavoured elsewhere to prove that the perfect being is possible.[9]

I had no intention, Sir, other than to write to you in a few words some minor thoughts on the Memoirs that you sent me; but the variety of the matters, the heat of the meditation, and the pleasure that I took from the generous intention of the Prince who is the patron of this work, carried me away. I beg your pardon for having taken so long, and I am, etc.

B. Optimism and Meliorism[10]

1. The elements of true piety, or, on the love of God over everything (early 1677–early 1678?)[11]

I call them *elements*, because they depend on demonstrations that are certain.

I talk of *piety*, not merely of moral virtues, because anyone is able to live rightly merely on account of human causes, such as education, custom, public peace, personal safety, and good repute. However we are concerned here with those things that we do or endure because of God.

To love is to be delighted by the happiness of someone, or to experience pleasure from the happiness of another. I define this as true love, which through its acknowledged cause differs from simple affection or even expedient friendship. I have sometimes discovered a notable use for this definition in discussion with a number of friends, who did not sufficiently grasp how the lover seeks the good of the beloved with no consideration of the wealth accruing to him; for it seems that whatever we do, we do it for our own good, and not for another's. Therefore how is it possible that we hope for the good of the beloved in itself? The difficulty is clearly resolved with the help of this definition, which shows that the happiness of the beloved is part of our own happiness. For just as we consider a painting excellent not because of some usefulness to us, but because of its own beauty, so we seek the happiness of the beloved for no other reason than that our acquaintance with it bathes us with pleasure. Just as it is evident from this corollary:

Corollary of the definition

The good of the beloved is desired in itself.

Demonstration:

The good of the beloved delights the lover,

from the hypothesis supposed in the definition of love, for we have defined love as being delighted by the happiness of another.

Whatever delights is to that extent desired in itself.

This proposition is evident, for things that delight us, even if they have no use, are desired nonetheless. And whatever things we desire, we desire them because they bring pleasure, or remove some pain. And if they bring about immediate pleasure, they are said to that extent to be desired in themselves, but if they serve only to obtain something else, which in fact produces pleasure, then they are sought only for the sake of the other thing. Therefore it is clear that things pleasant in themselves are desired, and useful things are desired because of the pleasant things.

Therefore the good of the beloved is sought in itself by the lover.

The beautiful is that, the contemplation of which is pleasant.
The good is that which contributes to delight.
Happiness is enduring joy.
Joy or delight is a feeling of perfection.
God is the most perfect being.
Perfection is the degree or quantity of reality.

Hence the most perfect is that which has the highest degree of reality. In other words, that being which contains as much reality and as many qualities and powers as is possible to belong to one subject at the same time. Hence it is understood that God has no limits of presence, of duration, of knowledge or of operation, and possesses as much of these as is possible to be possessed by one being.

Harmony is unity in variety.

Corollaries of these definitions

From many possible ways the more perfect is the one which brings it about that more reality exists in a given volume or receptacle.

This means more bodies in a given space, more motion in a given time, more forms in a given matter, and more qualities in a given subject.[12] Therefore the opposite of perfection is a vacuum in place, in time, in matter, in forms. The opposite is also redundant or superfluous to perfection, because ultimately it introduces a vacuum by consequence, for it removes space for more useful things and lacks its own space where it might more usefully be placed. Likewise, he who puts goods into a box is careful to arrange everything so that he wastes the least space; and nature itself collects liquid from hostile drought or squeezes a different fluid into a round drop, whereby it is exposed to the least amount of harm, because it encloses more matter within the same periphery. For the periphery alone, not that which is actually inside it, is exposed to harm. And the sphere is the most capacious of the shapes that have the same circumference.

Harmony is the perfection of thinkable things insofar as they are thinkable.

Harmony is when many things are reduced to a kind of unity. For where there is no variety, there is no harmony, and *the musician who always plays*: you know the rest.[13] In turn, where variety is without order, without proportion, without concord, there is no harmony. From this it is evident that however much greater is both the variety and the unity in variety, so much greater is the harmony. Hence the dissonances themselves increase the loveliness, if they are unexpectedly reduced to concord with other dissonances. Symmetry is the same. Now from this it is clearly evident that harmony is the perfection of thinkability. For in the preceding corollary it was said that the more perfect is that in which there is more reality. But thinking is also a kind of reality, and so much the greater because things are multiplied in a certain way by thought, for individual minds contain some representation of the whole world. Hence a more perfect manner of thinking is where one act of thinking extends to many things simultaneously, for in this way there is more reality in that thought. This is done, however, with the help of relations, for a relation is a kind of unity in multiplicity. And kinds of relations are the connections and reasons of things among themselves, proportions and proportionalities. Harmony results from everything in a given object taken together. Therefore the more relations (the aggregate of which is harmony) there are in a thinkable object, the more reality, or what is the same, the more perfection there is in the thought. Therefore it follows that harmony is the perfection of thinkable things, insofar as they are thinkable.

The great axiom

There is nothing without a reason.

Or, what is the same, nothing exists without there being some reason that can be given (at least by the omniscient) why it exists rather than not, and why it is thus rather than otherwise. From which it follows that, in itself and absolutely speaking, nothing is indifferent, as the indifference of things is merely an invention of our ignorance, as too is what heathens called chance. But in truth, someone will say, if there is nothing without a reason then there will be no first cause and no ultimate end. We must answer that, indeed, there is nothing without a reason, but that does not mean that there is nothing without a cause. For a cause is the reason for a thing outside of the thing, or its reason of production, but it is possible that the reason for a thing is inside the thing itself. And this is the case in all those things which are necessary, like the truths of mathematics which contain their reason in themselves; likewise God, who alone is the actual reason for the existence of actual things.

Definitions

The will is the judgement concerning good and evil.

That men understand this definition of 'will' is apparent from their modes of expression, in which if the definition is substituted for the thing defined then the sense will be evident to them. Hence we say everyone seeks the good and avoids the bad. No one wants evil on the grounds that it is evil. We will what we think is good, and conversely what we think is good is what we will. If anyone rejects this notion of the will, he is using the term in a way that is different from the one which men are accustomed to, and perhaps he will not even be able to say what it is to will something.

Judgement is practical thought, or the thought together with the endeavour to act.

This is evidently the distinction between simple thought, or consideration, imagination, representation, and judgement, because he who has some judgement is ready to act in some manner which conforms to this judgement. Whoever is persuaded that there is a fire in the furnace will certainly not insert his hand, as long as he is in control of his mind and his own actions. Whoever believes that he is the strongest and wisest critic of his own actions will certainly not sin as long as he has this judgement keeping watch within his mind. Hence it is clear that belief, i.e. a judgement, cannot exist without works, i.e. charity, or the attempt to do good works.

If anyone now substitutes the definition of 'judgement' in the definition of 'will', he will see that the will is the thinking about good and evil together with the endeavour to act; which agrees with the expression of those who say the will is the very last act of deliberation. For deliberation is an uncertainty, together with an inquiry, about the good and evil of some action or of some present omission. As long as we deliberate we are not yet ready to act; however when the inquiry and uncertainty are both over, only then have we established in earnest what we must do, and from that very moment onwards we endeavour to dispose ourselves and everything outside us for action.

But if anyone should prefer to say that the will is not the judgement of good and evil, but is the very endeavour to act which follows immediately from the judgement, I shall not dispute with him provided that he recognizes that the endeavour arises from the judgement. For an endeavour to act which does not originate from knowledge is irrational. Such is that endeavour to debase ourselves, which we feel in ourselves, not from a judgement of the mind, but from the burdensome nature of the body.

Even God discovers that some things are good, or better than others.

For God is endowed with will; the will is under the rule of the good.

Alternatively: every act of God is as a result of knowledge, every act as a result of knowledge is voluntary, every voluntary act is the cause of some good or evil.

Alternatively: some things are more perfect than others, as we have shown above; therefore they are more pleasant for the one who knows them (as God does), by the definition of pleasure. Therefore they are better, for the good is pleasant, or rather it contributes to what is pleasing.

Someone will say

God is the cause of things, and therefore is the cause of the goodness which is in them. Therefore his will is prior to the goodness of things.

The response is easy: God is the cause of the existence of things, but not of their essence, and to that extent he will also be the cause of the existence of the good, but not of the goodness which he discovers in the essence itself when thinking about it. In the same way God is the cause when some triangle exists, but he is not the cause of the nature of the triangle, nor of its properties. For instance it is absurd to say that God has given this privilege to the circle (i.e. to the figure having all outermost points equidistant from one middle point), that it is the most capacious of all the plane shapes of the same periphery (or which can be contained within the same circumference line). For it has this property because of its own nature, and the contrary implies contradiction. However if anyone says that God has given the circle its own nature, he surely doesn't know what he is saying. To what do I turn? To the circle itself. Therefore it is necessary that the circle is already something and endowed with a certain nature before anything is ascribed to it. So such things can be said, but they make no sense at all.

Moreover, if anyone insists that it follows from this that God is not the cause of everything, I shall answer that God is the cause of everything which exists outside himself, but not the cause of his own understanding, and hence not of the ideas exhibiting the essences of things, which are found in him.

Out of all the possible ways in which the universe or series of things is able to exist, one way is the most perfect, and that way is without doubt the one that really exists.

Given the most perfect being, namely God (as I now suppose), that the most perfect operation is that of the most perfect being, and that the world is the work of God, then the world is the most perfect, and hence no other series of things can be imagined which is more perfect than this one.

Alternatively: things have as much possibility as they have reality (for the essence of a rose in winter is the same thing as its possibility of existence) therefore those things that have the most possibility are without doubt those that exist in actuality, since they have the most reality, i.e. according to the definition of perfection they are the most perfect.

Alternatively: if this is not so, no reason can be given why this series of things should exist rather than any other. For certainly more series can be imagined, and it should not be thought that all possibles exist. For who would believe that no story can be imagined that will not have existed somewhere, or is not going to exist? But from many series it is necessary that one stands out ahead of the others, otherwise why should that exist rather than any of the others? But it will stand out because of its perfection; and the more perfect will be chosen, because God, the author of things, is certainly the most perfect.

Alternatively: since something exists rather than nothing, it is necessary that something is contained in the essence itself, or the possibility from which actual existence follows, and hence reality or possibility possesses a certain propensity to exist. Hence when many possibles obstruct each other, or when they are not able to co-exist, the one which contains more of reality, i.e. the one which is the most perfect, will exist.

All these demonstrations, if anyone examines them with care, come back to the same thing: for they show that this total series of past, present and future things taken together was chosen by God ahead of other possibles, because the most perfect cannot fail to please the wisest being, and what has pleased the most powerful being cannot fail to exist.

Because certain possibles exist, when they were equally able not to exist, it follows that 'possibility' is a certain disposition to exist rather than not to exist.

It is rather like this: existing possibles must differ in some way from the non-existing ones, which is the reason why they exist rather than others. This distinction must consist in something very general, but the most general distinction of the possibles is their very degree of reality, or quantity of essence. In fact it seems that two general distinctions can be supposed: one is the quantity of reality, the other is the quantity of possibility; but it seems that the quantity of reality and possibility differ only as something reciprocal, for the less reality each thing has the easier it is to see this. However we shall rightly conclude as follows: since there is something rather than nothing, it is necessary that there is a greater reason for existing rather than not existing. Once this is assumed, a reason must be given why all things do not exist. Because this cannot happen, it follows that as many things as possible exist.

2. On the continuous increase in the perfection of the world (March 1689–March 1690?)[14]

All things considered, I believe that the world continuously increases in perfection and does not go around in a circle as if by a revolution, for thus there would be no final cause. And although in God there is no pleasure, there is still in him something analogous to pleasure, so that he rejoices in the continuous advance of his plans. But there would be no pleasure, but torpor, if I remained in the same state, no matter how excellent. Happiness requires perpetual progress to new pleasures and perfections. Indeed all things are present to God as it were, and he embraces everything in himself. Nevertheless the execution requires time, and he did not have to achieve the greatest things immediately, otherwise there would be no more change, nor should they preserve the same perfection, otherwise there would be nothing further to achieve. The universe is similar to a plant or animal, in that it tends towards maturity. But this is the difference, that it never comes to the greatest degree of maturity, and also that it never goes back or falls into decline.

3. Whether the world increases in perfection (1694–1696?)[15]

The question is whether the whole world increases or decreases in perfection, or whether in fact it always preserves the same perfection, as I rather think, even if the different parts variously exchange perfection between themselves, so that it is mutually transferred. If the perfection of the world remains the same, some substances cannot continually increase in perfection without others continually decreasing in perfection. A substance increasing in perfection either increases continuously, or increases and decreases in turn, but only to the extent that it can be recognized to have increased more than it has decreased. If any substance progresses in perfection to infinity, whether directly or by interposed regressions, it is necessary that it can now be assigned a maximum degree of perfection below which it will never descend in the future, and in turn, after some time has elapsed, another degree of perfection can be assigned which is greater than the former. However it is not therefore necessary that the highest degree of ascent should always be moved forward. In which case it is necessary that the lowest degree of ascent within a given time, although it always moves forward, nevertheless attains a certain limit, or finally reaches the highest point of ascent, in which case the substance would then preserve the same degree of perfection forever. If the lowest degree at any time ceases to move forward, or at least has a limit beyond which it does not ascend, but the highest degree of ascent always moves forward, there is progress towards infinite perfection; but it is then perfect when the lowest descent likewise has no limit, and there is no ascent beyond.

But if a substance descends to infinity below any degree whatever, and also ascends below any degree whatever, it will still be seen to ascend if it ascends more than it descends.

Shall we say that the world increases by a necessary power, because souls are influenced by everything in the past? For, as we have demonstrated elsewhere, no perfect oblivion is granted to souls; even if we do not remember distinctly, nevertheless the whole that we now perceive consists of parts, into which all preceding actions enter. So should souls always progress over time towards more clearly expressed thoughts? If it cannot happen that a perfection is given which cannot be increased, it follows that the perfection of the universe always increases; for thus it is more perfect than if it did not increase. Supreme happiness does not consist in a certain highest degree, but in the continuous increase of joy. The greatest being does not increase in perfection, because it is outside time and change and it includes the present and future equally.

4. Letter to André Morell (29 September 1698)[16]

I am effectively of the opinion that God could not do better than he does, and that all the imperfections we think we find in the world only originate from our ignorance. We also do not have the right point of view to judge of the beauty of things. It is a bit like in astronomy, where the motion of the planets appears to be a pure confusion when one looks at it from the Earth, but if we were in the sun we would find before our very eyes this beautiful arrangement of the system which Copernicus has discovered by dint of reasoning. As the smallest bodies are, so to speak, small worlds full of marvellous creatures, we should not imagine that there are barren parts, absolutely speaking, even though they seem barren to us. But the fact is that we must consider that we are not the measure of things, especially in the state we are in at present. Sins themselves are only evil for those who sin, and absolutely speaking they increase the perfection of things, just as shadows are good in a painting in order to enhance the light. *Deus non permitteret malum, nisi majus bonum procuraret ex malo* [God would not permit evil unless he could procure a greater good from evil]. It even seems to me that these truths are so important that unless we fully understand them we can neither truly esteem nor truly love God, the indifference attributed to him being absolutely incompatible with a perfect wisdom and goodness.

5. Letter to Louis Bourguet (5 August 1715)[17]

Two hypotheses can be formed, one that nature is always equally perfect, the other that it always increases in perfection. If it is always equally perfect, but in variable ways, it is more likely that it did not have a beginning. But if it always increases in perfection (supposing that it is not possible to give to it all its perfection at once) the matter could still be explained in two ways, namely by the ordinates of hyperbola B or by those of triangle C. According to the hypothesis of the hyperbola, there would be no beginning, and the instants or states of the world would have been increasing in perfection from all eternity; but according to the hypothesis of the triangle, there would have been a beginning. The hypothesis of equal perfection would be that of the rectangle A. As yet, I do not see a way of showing demonstratively by pure reason which of these we should choose. But even though the state of the world, taken in any instant whatever, could never be absolutely perfect according to the hypothesis of increase, nevertheless the whole actual sequence would not fail to be the most perfect of all those possible, because God always chooses the best possible.

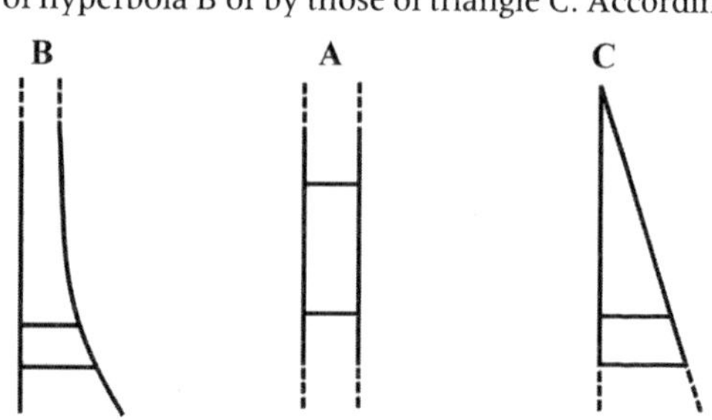

6. Letter to Louis Bourguet (mid-to-late March 1716)[18]

The change of ordinates in the rectangle is always such that the posterior keeps the lines of the anterior, and it does not follow that this introduces an increase in perfection; for if there remains something of the preceding state, then something of it does not remain. Even if the universe were always equally perfect, it will never be sovereignly perfect, for it always changes and gains new perfections, although it loses some old ones. With regard to the hypothesis of the hyperbola, it does not follow either that what has no beginning necessarily exists, for it could always have been voluntarily produced by the sovereign being. Thus it is not that easy to decide between the three hypotheses, and we must still engage in a lot of meditation in order to come to any conclusion about them.

7. Letter to Louis Bourguet (3 April 1716)[19]

As for the big question, if it is possible to demonstrate by reason which hypothesis, namely that of the rectangle, triangle or hyperbola, is preferable in the constitution of the universe, I believe that we would have to adhere to a rigorous argument in good form in order to decide . . .

You are right, Sir, to say that from the fact that finite beings are infinite in number it does not follow at all that their system must receive at the start all the perfection of which it is capable. For if this consequence was right, the hypothesis of the rectangle would be demonstrated.

I also believe that the result of that is truly infinite, and must not be compared to an infinite sequence of numbers whose sum is finite. But one infinity, to speak according to our capacity, is greater than another, for example, the sum of this series

$\frac{1}{1} + \frac{1}{2} + \frac{1}{3} + \frac{1}{4} + \frac{1}{5}$ and so on to infinity

is infinite and surpasses every assignable number; but nevertheless the sum of this other series

$\frac{1}{1} + \frac{1}{1} + \frac{1}{1} + \frac{1}{1} + \frac{1}{1}$ and so on to infinity

is infinitely greater than the previous one. Thus the perfection of the system, although infinite, would not for all that be the greatest possible, but would always approach it.

Ideas or essences are all founded on a necessity independent of wisdom, fittingness and choice; but existences are dependent on them.

Even if the rectangle has obtained, nothing produced by the eternal wisdom would be coeternal with it, since its productions always change. A necessary production must not be subject to any change.

Every state of the universe is always limited in perfection, even if the preceding state were to be equal in perfection to the subsequent one; for both together embrace more perfections than the one alone. It is also for that reason that change is appropriate, in order that there should be more kinds or forms of perfection, even if they would be equal in degree. Even so, in God the idea of the work always precedes the work; the present state of things was always known beforehand.

8. Letter to Louis Bourguet (2 July 1716)[20]

If the rectangle has obtained in the order of things, we would have to admit that the productions of the divine wisdom would be coeternal with that divine wisdom, and that each substance would have been eternal with respect to what precedes it, just as I believe that they are all eternal with respect to what follows.

C. Sin and Evil[21]

1. On sin and original sin (April–October 1686?)[22]

In the first place, I think that there is a most perfect substance which we call 'God', and it is unique, eternal, omnipresent, omniscient and omnipotent. All other things are created by this substance by the most beautiful plan and are conserved by a sort of continual production. Therefore the doctrine of those who imagine that God is corporeal, finite, circumscribed by space, and ignorant of future contingents, absolute or conditional, should not be tolerated at all. And hence I greatly disapprove of certain Antitrinitarians and those like them, who have not even left intact this head of faith and think things that are very unworthy of God.

Further, this supreme intelligence has made other minds in order that he might be glorified, and he governs them by the most just of plans, so that the one who understands the whole plan of this divine management will discover a model of the most perfect commonwealth, in which the wise man can want for nothing nor have any wish unfulfilled. Therefore we must shun those who conceive God as a certain supreme power from which all other things emanate, but indiscriminately, by a kind of necessity of existence, without any choice of the beautiful or the good, as if these notions were either arbitrary or not established in nature but only by human imagination.

Therefore God is not only the greatest author of things, but also the best leader and even legislator of minds, but he demands nothing from his subjects than that their souls be sincerely affected and endowed with right intention, persuaded about this very beneficence and most just government, and about the beauty and goodness of the most lovable Lord of all, and hence that they do not merely fear the power of the supreme and all-seeing monarch, but are assured of its benevolence, and finally, which covers all these other things, that they are aroused by the love of God above everything.

Indeed, those who understand these things, fix them deep inside their mind and express them in their life, they never grumble about the divine will, knowing that *all things work together for the good for those who love God,*[23] and just as they are content with the past, so they endeavour, with regard to the future, to do everything which they judge to agree with the presumed will of God. But his will demands, with the rewards and punishments that are proposed, that each person adorn his own Sparta[24] and cultivate where he is placed in the likeness of the garden of the first man, and in imitation of the divine goodness that he spread his own beneficence to nearby things, but especially to every man he meets just as if he were his neighbour, observing a proper measure of justice, because among the creatures with which we interact none is more excellent than man, and it pleases God for him to be as perfect as possible.

Therefore if all minds were always to reflect on this and pursue it in their actions, they would without question live happily. But since it is evident that this neither always is nor has been the case, the question is how has sin, and through sin misery, entered into the world, since God, the author of all good, cannot be in any way the cause of sin. We must therefore consider that in all creatures, however excellent they are, there is a certain innate and original limitation or imperfection before every sin, which makes them fallible. And it is in this sense that we should understand what Job seems to have meant when saying that the holiest angels are not exempt from defect, that is, from imperfection.[25] And this is not inconsistent[26] with original justice and with our being made in the image of God. For inasmuch as a rational creature is adorned with perfection, it has this from the divine image, but inasmuch as it is limited and lacking certain perfections, to that extent it contains privation or nothingness. St. Augustine's opinion also comes down to this: that the cause of evil is not from God but from nothingness, that is, not from the positive but from the privative, that is, from the very limitation of creatures that we have discussed.[27]

Although it was possible for God to create only minds that, although they could fall, would not fall, nevertheless it pleased his inscrutable wisdom to produce this order of things that we know from experience, in which some possible minds (which involve in their own possible concept or in the idea of them that exists in God a certain series of free actions, of divine auxiliaries, and likewise of faith, and charity, and of eternal blessedness, or the opposite of these) were selected from innumerable others that were equally possible and admitted to existence, i.e. created, such as Adam, who was to be an exile, Peter, the prince of the apostles, who was to be a denier, confessor and martyr, Judas, who was to be a traitor, etc. And doubtless because God foresaw and permitted the evil which enters into some people, he knew how to turn it into a much greater good than would have existed without this evil, so that this series would ultimately be, all in all, more perfect than all the others. Thus Adam's fall was redeemed with an immeasurable gain in perfection through the incarnation of the Word, and Judas's treason through the redemption of humankind.

Therefore, when some angels fell through pride, as it seems, and when afterwards the first man, seduced by an evil angel, also fell through concupiscence – the former being diabolical sin, the latter bestial sin – original sin invaded humankind through the first parent, that is, a certain depravity was contracted which renders men slow to act rightly, quick to act wickedly, since their understanding is obscured and their senses have more influence. But even if a pure soul emanates from God (for a traduction of souls makes no sense), nevertheless by virtue of its union with the body, original sin, i.e. the disposition to sin, arises in it as a result of the vice of the parents, or through the connection with external things, although we can identify no moment when it was free from defect, and had to be inserted into a corrupted body. And so all have become *children of wrath*[28] and *concluded under sin,*[29] to go head first into ruin unless they are assisted by God's great grace.

I would not extend the power of original sin so far as to say that infants who have committed no actual sin will be damned, in the way that many people claim, for under God, the just judge, no one can be wretched without his own offence.

Actual sins are of two kinds; some are venial, which must be expiated by a temporal punishment, others are mortal, which merit eternal ruin. And this division is not only ancient, but also seems consistent with divine justice, and I cannot agree with those who, like the Stoics, consider all sins nearly equal, or worthy of eternal damnation by the greatest punishment. But unlike the others, mortal sins are those committed by an evil mind and against the express conscience and the principles of virtue innate in the mind. For as those who withdraw from this life badly disposed towards God are revived without having had any further external sensations, they seem to proceed with the road undertaken and to preserve the state of the soul in which their minds were seized, and because of that they are separated from God, whence by a sort of consequence they fall into the greatest unhappiness of the soul, and hence damn themselves, so to speak.

Now all men, being born in sin, and not yet regenerated by the grace of the Holy Spirit, are apt to commit mortal sins as soon as they have attained the use of reason, or at least they are until they are restrained by some singular grace of God; for all men are informed by their conscience of what is right and wrong, and yet they are repeatedly overcome by their passions. And hence the human race would perish were it not for the fact that God formed a plan from eternity for its redemption or expiation, a plan worthy of his mercy and his ineffable wisdom and which is executed in his own time.

For we must hold as certain that God does not want the death of the sinner,[30] and desires that all men be saved,[31] not in fact with an absolute and irresistible will, but with a will ordered and circumscribed by certain laws; and hence we must hold that he assists each person as far as the rules of his wisdom and justice permit.

And in fact the things we have said till now are almost all evident from the light of reason itself; but it is only from God's revelation that we have been able to learn about the secret plan of the divine counsel with regard to the restitution of men.

We must therefore bear in mind that God is not only the First Substance, the Author and Preserver of all other things, but also that he is the most perfect mind, and on that account he is imbued with a moral quality, and enters into a sort of society with other minds. In this society God presides as a supreme monarch over all of his subjects, who are collected into the most perfect commonwealth that we may call the city of God.

2. Can the bad outcomes of wicked actions be ascribed to wickedness? (1696–1697?)[32]

The question pertains to my theodicy whether unfortunate outcomes really and truly are due to sins, as they are thought to be by historians and preachers, good men, and common people whether pious or superstitious.

In this matter there is truly a certain confusion of views. I remember Tasso, in his unpublished notes on the Annals of Baronius, although inclining towards the true faith of the Roman Church, nevertheless rebuked and ridiculed that bad habit of certain historians who assign to providence their own dispositions, implying that misfortunes happen to certain leaders because they have thought and acted, I shall not say wickedly, but scarcely according to the custom of the Roman curia. Nevertheless it is worthwhile to ask whether unfortunate events may be ascribed not so much to the imprudence of men (which no one denies), but rather to sin and wickedness, in cases where men have not failed in themselves but are overthrown by a greater power, although even imprudence can sometimes be considered as a kind of blinding inflicted from on high, especially when it has exceeded what is usual. There are examples of this when someone who has broken a treaty and then lost the resultant war seems to declare to himself and to others that he will learn justice; for example, as Ladislaus King of Hungary and Poland said:

As the Romans did for Cannae, I have made Varna famous for defeat
For mortals to learn not to violate trust;
If popes had not ordered me to break the treaty,
The country of Pannonia would not know the Scythian yoke.[33]

For my part, where justice is doubtful and controversial, I say that an outcome should not be considered as a sentence pronounced by God; and I believe that those who once said in Ordali that disputes had to be decided by a battle that was to be joined by divine judgement itself were putting God to the test, although they were acting imprudently rather than wickedly. But where the depravity of a deed is indisputable, and it is followed by a bad outcome, what shall we say then? At any rate it is often said against this that the wicked are happy, so that if you undertook an induction of examples and carried out a census of histories you would not so boldly claim that the wicked are more often punished than (I will not say the unconvicted) those that have been made happy. But my question ought not to be put to the atheist and the one who overthrows providence, but to a man convinced of the highest wisdom and power of God and the most just administration of things. For it is evident that far too often punishments are deferred to another life, so that in these times wickedness seems to prevail as though it had a privilege in the kingdom of this world. So success could be seen as a sign of an evil cause, like the wise man who, when he was applauded by a crowd, became afraid that he had said something bad.

Therefore shall we order those preachers or moralistic historians to get out of our sight, even though they take account of genuine and not imaginary sins? Or shall we tolerate them, showing a kind of pious dishonesty that we defend on the grounds that it will be useful to men? And shall we decide to say that sin is indeed the cause of unhappiness or one of its causes?

It seems to me that this final opinion is the truest, since it is certain that God, and not an evil genius, is the director of things, and he doesn't do anything rashly; all things come back to some infallible calculation and are adjusted to each other by eternal decrees. Someone will urge, not implausibly, that this statement is made truthfully but in vain. For on account of the universal connection of all things, even virtues are among the causes of future unhappiness, not because anyone suffers on account of justice, or where there is a similar cause, by the reward being postponed to the future; but in general, i.e. adverse events arise that are no more from sin than from virtue. However to meet this deeper objection we must understand that all things work together, but for very different reasons. And when we are thinking about moral interests and the actions of the wise, we should consider as causes those influences on the effect that arise through reasons of wisdom and of the will, and not those that influence the effect through the principle of individuation or contingency (which some call material necessity, although that is somewhat improper talk), or have been brought about through the general working-together of things. Indeed eternal wisdom connects both these things, but this wisdom transcends the grasp of the finite mind and we cannot nor should not trace it back into its reasons. In this context emphasis should be given to causes that act by themselves, because most people run these together with the laws of universal principles, perhaps not with necessary or essential laws, but at least with presumptive or natural laws, unlike jurisconsults who distinguish essential and natural laws. When God produces bodies naturally he undoubtedly makes them regular, uniform, suitable for their function whether as animals or planets in the sky. The only exception is when he has to act otherwise because of a mutual obstruction; although even then beauty of the whole is evident, as my demonstrations about the laws of motion show. Therefore God punishes evils and metes out rewards naturally, that is, from reasons of wisdom, or rather from certain universal principles (which perform the same role in moral matters as laws of motion in physics), and immediately, if the greater reasons demanded by the concourse of other moral matters permit it; moral, I say, not natural. For in this matter the most excellent Malebranche did not see the issue clearly, because he thought that moral matters are disturbed by the natural, when in fact the laws of any kingdom are perfect in themselves and have inviolate success. But if it is not possible immediately then God will surely punish as soon as conveniently possible, and the person will be brought to punishment by a natural impetus: that in fact is what Holy Scripture insinuates when it says that God hates sin. Indeed this was so from the very beginning, when from the infinity of possible worlds he chose the order of things in which the fewest possible sins would happen, and which would be compensated by punishment and correction as early as possible. And so it should be considered most certain that misfortune after wickedness is to be ascribed to that wickedness as it is that death following malignant fever is to be ascribed to that fever, even if the knowledge of doctors was so great that most fevers of this kind could be cured.

3. Letter to Isaac Jacquelot (6 October 1706)[34]

In the question of the origin of evil, the one who would want to bring an invincible objection against the goodness and wisdom of God would have to prove, for example, that evil could be avoided without losing some more considerable amount of good. But in order to prove this thesis, it would not be sufficient to say that someone else could not prove the contrary, nor show the connection of these evils with greater goods, because it is enough that we can say that this connection is possible until the opposite is proved, which people must be careful not to claim, inasmuch as it would lead to an absurdity, that is to say, that God would not have acted in accordance with the most perfect wisdom. For as it is true that there is an infinitely perfect God who has permitted evil, we must say with St. Augustine that he did it for a greater good, although it is beyond the forces of human reason to show *a priori* and in detail in what this good consists. For it is sufficient to know roughly and *a posteriori* that this must be the case, because evil actually happened and God exists.

4. Letter to Louis Bourguet (late 1712)[35]

When I say that there is an infinity of possible worlds, I mean those which do not imply a contradiction, just as one can invent stories that never exist and which are nevertheless possible. In order to be possible it is sufficient that there is intelligibility; but for existence there must be a prevalence of intelligibility or order; because there is order to the extent that there is more to observe in a multitude.

I do not believe that a world without evil, preferable in order to ours, is possible; otherwise it would have been preferred. We must believe that the mixture of evil has produced the greatest possible good: otherwise the evil would not have been permitted.

The combination of all the tendencies to the good has produced the best: but as there are goods that are incompatible together, this combination and this result can introduce the destruction of some good, and as a result some evil.

Notes

1 See also I.A.3, II.B.2.

2 A VI iv 18–19. Latin.

3 *a parte rei, seu ut vocant objectivae*. I have throughout translated *a parte rei* as 'objectively' except here, where I render it as 'in reality' in order to avoid the tautology 'objectively or as they say objectively'. However Leibniz's use of *seu* between *a parte rei* and *objectivae* indicates that he considered the expression *a parte rei* to be equivalent to 'objectively'.

4 Plato, *Laws*, 894b–896a.

5 A VI iv 17. Latin.

6 A II i 390–3. Latin.

7 In the margin Leibniz wrote here: 'If a necessarily existing being is possible, it will certainly exist, for if a necessarily existing being does not exist it will be impossible because it implies contradiction that some being exists necessarily and yet does not exist. Therefore the issue comes down to this, that we show that a necessary being, or an essence from which existence follows, is possible.

(The whole issue comes down to this one word: If a necessarily existing being is possible, it actually exists. For if it will not exist it is certainly possible that it does not exist. Therefore it is impossible that it is necessary, i.e. that it is not able to not exist. Therefore an actually non-existing necessary being is impossible. Therefore if a necessary being is possible, it will actually exist.)

A necessary being is proved by that to exist and to be possible at the same time, because otherwise all things are contingent. If all things are contingent then they were able to be otherwise by an equal reason, i.e. it is false that nothing exists without a reason.

If a necessarily existing being is possible, then its essence can be understood to include necessary existence. If that essence is A, I say that the being endowed with essence A exists. For if it does not exist it is not necessary that it exists. Therefore its essence does not include necessary existence, which is contrary to the hypothesis, for it either implies impossibility or it is impossible. Therefore if a being endowed with essence A does not exist, it will be impossible. But essence A includes necessary existence. Therefore if a necessarily existing being does not exist it will be impossible, or if a necessary being is possible, it exists. Which was to be demonstrated.'

8 G IV 405–6. French. This text, part of a letter sent to François Pinsson in late June 1701, was published in the September/October 1701 issue of *Journal de Trévoux*.
9 See 'That a most perfect being is possible' in DSR 91–5.
10 See also I.A.3, I.A.5, II.C.2.
11 A VI iv 1357–64. Latin.
12 Leibniz deleted the following sentence here: 'Hence the sphere is a more perfect shape because it encloses more matter within the same periphery than any other shape.'
13 'The musician who always plays on the same string, is laughed at.' Horace, *Ars Poetica*, 355.
14 A VI iv 1642. Latin.
15 Gr 95. Latin.
16 A I xvi 162. French.
17 G III 582–3. French.
18 G III 589. French.
19 G III 591–3. French.
20 G III 595. French.
21 See also I.A.3, III.A.3.
22 A VI iv 2357–60. Latin. From Leibniz's *Examination of the Christian Religion*.
23 Romans 8.28.
24 An illusion to Euripides *Telephus* (fragment 73).
25 Job 4.18.
26 Reading *pugnat* for *puguat*.
27 St. Augustine, *City of God*, Book 14, Chapter 13.
28 Ephesians 2.3.
29 Galatians 3.22.
30 A paraphrase of Ezekiel 33.11.
31 A paraphrase of 1 Timothy 2.4.
32 Gr 372–4. Latin.
33 This refers to the battle of Varna in 1444, when the Turks ('Scythians') defeated the Hungarians and took over Central Europe (Pannonia).
34 Gr 66. French.
35 G III 558. French.

Index